Stress RELEASE
For Dogs: The Canine Emotional Detox

DIANE GARROD

CONTENTS

Introduction

"Since nearly everyone at sometime or other has tried, or wished
he knew how to train a dog, a cat, or some other animal, perhaps
the most useful way to explain the learning process is to describe
some simple experiments which the reader can perform himself."
-Skinner, 1951/1999, p.605

Working with challenging dogs, daily, it is my life's work that their emotional well-being is taken seriously. Stress is a natural part of a canine's life. It protects them from danger. Good stress (eustress) provides a sense of well-being and safety. It is when stress spikes go over threshold and take days to come down, or when stress goes over threshold and stays there that behavior problems arise.

The first person to discover stress was Scientist and Physician, Hans Selye, (1907-1982) introducing G.A.S., the **General Adaptation Syndrome** model (the process under which the body confronts stress) in 1936 showing in three phases of what the alleged effects of stress has on the body. In his work, Selye deemed *'the father of stress research,'* developed the theory that stress is a major cause of disease and chronic stress causes long-term chemical changes.

Early on, 1915, it was Dr. Walter B. Cannon who first developed the term fight or flight. Walter Cannon studied at Harvard University and stayed there to teach in the Department of Physiology. Although he was a physiologist by training, Dr. Cannon became interested in the physical reactions of his laboratory animals when under stress. While studying digestion in his animals, Dr. Cannon noticed that physical changes in the function of the stomach would occur when the animal was frightened or scared. He went on to study all the various physiological reactions to stress throughout the body.

In this book, you will discover that there are great benefits to releasing stress prior to implementing a behavior modification program. From sensory application to engaging the mind and brain in problem-solving activities, the Canine Emotional Detox (CED) provides the right combination of progressive elements to achieve stress release in challenging dogs in the form of a systematic process (Chapter 5, The Right Combination).

Ultimately the achievement of deep sleep is the goal. Once a stress release process has satisfactorily been completed then a force free behavior modification program is developed based on a detailed CED final analysis identifying patterns to help the individual dog move forward progressively and change emotional responses (CERs) while continuing stress release and keeping stress spikes within normal ranges.

Why Do A CED

The simple answer to why to do a CED is because it changes the dog from the inside outwardly. Feeling good internally, throughout body and brain, allows the dog to exhibit change outwardly. The feel-good chemicals grow, such as oxytocin, serotonin and the release or neutralization of the bad chemicals occur. Observing the patterns, the dog goes through allows for a customized behavior modification program that focuses on how a dog thinks, thereby keeping the process progressive, successful and results-oriented. Releasing stress is vital to allowing the dog to cope with real life effectively, to think through choices, make good decisions and to renew a relationship and bond that may have eroded due to behavioral challenges.

The CED is an intense 72-hour process and customized to the individual. The intensity is good and needed. It is like an intervention program for those suffering addictions and sometimes a dog's behavior will get worse before it gets better, especially in the second day. The body starts to feel different, better, but unfamiliar, if behavior has habituated.

What this book contains

The CED is not magic, it is not a recipe. The CED is based on physiology, neuroscience, and it is about changing the dog from the inside outwardly through a cleansing detox diet, evaluation of biologics such as waste, pH urine, respiration, weight, and muscle tension. It is about observing patterns of how a dog functions when presented with play and problem-solving. How a dog thinks has direct influence on the success of addressing challenges in a behavior modification program. This book is a workbook, a training manual for dog professionals working with highly stressed cases. Since it is the order of the process that relieves stress, skipping steps is not implementing the CED.

A new study in Plos One suggests it is okay to call oneself a pet parent, and that dogs bring joy much as children do. Researchers looked at brain scans of women who had at least one child between the ages of two and 10 and a dog for two or more years. The brain areas linked with emotion, reward and relationships lit up when they saw photos of their children and when they saw pictures of their dog. Besides offering affection, a dog can help with one's stress and heart health.

The CED allows the pet guardian to view their dog differently, implement activities with them and build a better bond and relationship all helping to move forward in a behavior modification and skills learning process. It can change the emotional bond in both species.

Ideally, the CED should precede behavior modification and skills in challenging dogs, but at the same time can be implemented any time during the process already in progress. If done in the right combination, it is very versatile. If you are reading this book, most likely you have a dog yourself, or a client dog that could use a stress release protocol. The following pages will show you how to do a CED properly and explain why and what happens internally and externally.

Dedication

FOR Chancellor who forced me to think deep and outside of the box and to find the answers to bringing a systematic stress release to client dogs and the world. Chancellor, my heart and soul dog, is the paw on my hand teaching me the missing link to working with challenging dogs and going beyond just diving into behavior modification before releasing stress. You were my teacher and muse, and your legacy will live on helping dogs around the world to thrive and live progressive, positive lives. (Chancellor's story appears in Chapter two)

For all dogs facing challenges daily and their pet guardians, trainers, veterinarians, foster homes, and rescues and to understand your lives are important in the scheme of things. You will teach us ever more than we will ever teach you.

Illustration by Sue VanEtten, Langley, WA

R.I.P 4/03/2004 to 1/24/2015, I will light a candle in memory and I will cry, I will smile, and I will be happy you were in my life. Your memory lives on.

Acknowledgements

It is interesting how stress is so misunderstood in dogs and that just the release of distress, acute or chronic, can be highly instrumental in creating an environment of learning and progressive results.

This book is different from others on stress in dogs because it identifies an exact protocol/system for releasing stress in challenging dogs. It is designed to precede a behavior modification program and in many cases, a skills applications process. To date, I must thank over 700 cases (permission-based cases). I am especially grateful to my dog Chancellor (Wyld Waves of Chance) for teaching me to look beyond tradition, beyond methods and techniques and to explore the unknown. Chancellor's reactivity to humans, grand mal seizures, and way over-the-top behaviors are key to the development of the Canine Emotional Detox: A stress release protocol for challenging dogs. His paw, on my hand, guided my writing. Chancellor passed away 1/24/2015 close to his eleventh birthday, 4/03/2004. His legacy will live on, and the work he started continues.

This book is a compilation of research, expressed knowledge, and the inspiration and ideas of those who have studied stress, cognition, emotion, relaxation, touch, and mental activity in dogs before me. It is my hope this book will grow, expand and help a new generation of trainers with a stress protocol that is the gold standard and guide creating knowledge that stress release should be done prior to a behavior modification program when working with highly challenging dogs. The growing audiences of people committed to force free, fear free, positive rehabilitation of canines and other pets is the underlying message. The greatest rewards of working with challenging dogs are seeing them change on a daily basis with an understanding that the rewards come after we learn to accept and respect the individual realizing there is not a one-size-fit-all method. This fact is what made this book difficult to write, because it is about the individual, the customization of the process that reaps the best rewards for success. Each canine is as different as a fingerprint or a snowflake and there are no recipes, but there can be a systematic process bringing results. Without Chancellor, without the many cases of real-life dogs and their pet guardians, as well as the trainers who embraced the process, this book would not exist. For that I thank you all, as many dogs will thrive in human environments, not just survive, because of you.

I want to thank my husband, Carl, for understanding all the long hours and effort that was put into compiling this book. He is a saint and often fixed meals, cleaned the house, and got me away from the computer for an outing. He kept encouraging me to "Just finish the book."

Thanks to Angelica Schmitz Steinker, M.Ed., DBC-A, CDBC, DBCT, CAP2, PTC-A, Courteous Canine and Jan Pimm Casey, of Golden Hearts Dog Training, LLC, Lutz, Florida for believing in me and asking me to do my very first workshop on the CED in Lutz, Florida. Thanks to my dear friend and colleague, now retired to South Carolina, Leslie Clifton, PMCT, CPDT-KA for being the first trainer to embrace and use the CED with a passion. She says, *"For pet guardians the CED is a life changing process. For the pets, the CED can be literally lifesaving. Highly recommended for any troubled dog."* Leslie Clifton, PMCT, CPDT-KA, South Carolina.

Thanks also goes to Lynn Honneckman, DVM, Veterinarian Behaviorist, Florida (quoted on the back cover of this book); Vickie Aquino Ronchette, Braveheart Dog Training in Pleasanton, California; Ana Melara, Training with Grace, Denver, Colorado; HEARTland Positive Dog Trainer's Alliance, Kansas City, Missouri; APDT Australia team and all who have held workshops and seminars on this topic.

A huge thanks to creating many illustrations in the book, Carol Byrnes, Author of "What is my dog saying"; "What is my dog saying at the dog park" and "What is my cat saying" interactive PowerPoint CDs, available at www.dogwise.com. Carol is owner of Diamonds in the Ruff dog training, Spokane, Washington State. Also, to Sue VanEtten, former client, and creator of the sketch of Chancellor, and her husband Dan Peterson, writer, photographer, author of ten books, who put their dog Duncan through the CED. Illustration at end of book is created by my good friend, former client Lynda McCormick, Freeland, WA.

Thanks to Melissa Alexander, Click for Joy, Kathy Cascade, PCT-A, physical therapist and Tellington Touch Instructor, and Jennifer White, Laughing Dog and i2iK9 for helping me to see the potential in Chancellor and to provide guidance. Melissa recommended that I see Jennifer White and not listen to the other bad advise I was being given to take him to academies and aversive trainers. As a result, the CED was born as Chancellor made a smooth transition with force free methods. Thank you for your insights, expertise and for the experience you brought to the situation when I thought I was at a dead end. Neither you nor Chancellor let me give up and opened doors to further exploration of the issue.

As a founding member of the Pet Professional Guild (PPG – www. petprofessionalsguild.com) my thanks go to Niki Tudge, Founder, for presenting CED process at their first conference in Tampa, FL, and to Susan Nielson for articles in the association's publication Barks from the Guild as a regular writer. In addition, thanks to Tawzer Dog for filming the basics of the CED at this conference still available today in DVD at www.tawzer-dogs.com. It is a perfect compliment to the book.

Thanks to all pet guardians, and their trainers (especially Ira Vaculik, Canine Behavior Counselor, Germany, talking about Lobo's success in the Forward of this book) who completed the CED successfully, and all permission-based guardians completing the CED, as this book could not be written without the input you and your dogs provided showing time and again that releasing stress is a key component to addressing, transforming and changing behavior. With over 700 completed permission-based cases (at this writing, as CEDs and research will be ongoing), listing all names is not possible, but many of the dogs will appear within the pages of this book. Your dogs will bring hope and change to others.

More praise for The Canine Emotional Detox

"I love learning the CED process. It brings more understanding to the relationship on how each of us, in our own unique way, communicate. It is not only about seeing the dog for who they are but seeing the guardian's views and responses to their dog. It is a learning process for both. If I were to just do a case without doing a CED first, I probably would have left out some important steps because doing a CED you get to see patterns, likes & dislikes, how the dog processes information, are they chronically stressed, clues on health in their poop, how does the owner view their dog, and more. The direction is much clearer now on how to approach a behavior modification training plan, which saves everyone time and gets to the root of the cause."-**Patricia Calderone, CPDT-KA, DN-FSG1, Owner, Clicker Canines**

"So many people have the motivation to work on their dog's emotional and behavioral issues but do not know where to begin. Diane Garrod's CED program provides the perfect start." **Emily Larlham, Dogmantics Training**

While this book focuses on dogs, the CED has been used with cats, parrots, and children. For example, a use of some elements of the CED were done in a classroom of challenging children in a New Zealand country school in early 2015. Here is the story of two teachers, who first worked through the CED with their own dogs, bringing respiration of one dog from 76 to 18 breaths per minute. A certified dog trainer and author, Maria Alomajan, Canine by Nature, worked with them throughout the process. The school sampling included approximately six children. Most came from very difficult homes where alcoholism, fighting, no money, no food, no sleep for the kids, no kindness, going to school without proper clothing, food, or care, were prevalent. The children had trouble concentrating or simply learning how to have positive relationships with fellow students. It was a light bulb moment for the teachers!

Here is the teacher's story told through Maria Alomajan's (who has done many stress release protocols with her New Zealand clients) words and with permission from the school's teachers.

"I want to share what a massive influence your work has been filtering through to children in a tiny country school. While working with their (a client's) dogs, I was discussing your process, the limbic system and applied behavior analysis (ABA). We played the shaping game, and they took it to work and played it as team building at a staff meeting and reported back that it was brilliant.

The amazing outcome, aside from all my time with them (the client,) aside from the positives for the two dogs they still live with, is that they decided they needed to do something for a handful of children who were really struggling at school. They needed to take more time to understand why they behaved certain ways and think about how they could help them. (The client, a teacher at the school) devised a program where when the kids arrived at school, instead of going to class they went to a quiet room, where they were fed and given a warm Milo (hot chocolate), where they just got to sit and listen to quiet music or read or have someone read to them. They discussed mindfulness and when the kids were ready, they went into their class. The results have been amazing!

The teachers jokingly asked if they were drugging the kids because they were so Zen-like when they joined in, no disrupting, doing their work, being proactive in asking other students for help if the teacher was not available. The other side of that was one boy who had been labeled as trouble, excelled, and asked if he could go straight to class now instead of his morning sessions because he had begun to enjoy school. Seems so obvious now that all schools should have such a program." **Maria Alomajan, Canine by Nature Author of "Dogs in Action: Working dogs and their stories" New Zealand**

There was one boy in the school for whom even the quiet time was too much for him because he never got to experience relaxation so he required a whole other level of care and they would just let him sit and read to him. Adding additional pieces as required by the individual in front of us, is also relevant to children. The revisions to fit certain situations to the cycle are indeed amazing and progressive. The boy who couldn't relax, showed he has chronic stress and that needs to be identified first, and/or something going on internally, such as in the brain, neurological system. It was a moment where the school could look at the reason for the behavior instead of just thinking the boy was being difficult. In CED case analysis, a very small percentage (10%) are chronically stressed and a lot more thought and work and stress release must occur to see results, however, the majority (90%) benefit right away. This also proved true in the country school.

"I love the structure the CED provides for both the dog and the trainer. It gives us a safe, controlled way to get to know each other that promotes relaxation and builds trust. Doing a CED makes it much easier to develop a training or B-Mod program that specifically meets the needs of that dog." **Cricket Mara, Pet guardian of The Pawsitive Dog, New Mexico USA**

"I love that it truly prepares the dog to begin a behavior modification plan as well as giving the trainer lots of valuable information about the dog." **Vicki Aquino Ronchette, Braveheart Dog Training, San Leandro, CA, USA**

"On Chai's 5th birthday, I was enjoying what that meant—AND what a contribution you made to our lives with your help. She is a different dog

today. Happily, I can say that after three months we fully weaned her off the Prozac. She is still Chai –with her terrier traits and personality based on her early life (and karma?) but she is not the emotionally tormented pup when we first contacted you. Just wanted to thank you for all you did of us and for what you do for others." **Kirkland, WA**

"When our daughter purchased Niamh, a GSP, the puppy lived happily in our home with our two older female Labrador Retrievers, Bronte and Amica. They both mothered Niamh. They played with her and allowed her to sleep cuddled up to them. Apart from being hyperactive, Niamh had demonstrated multiple signs of severe general anxiety from a young age, but this did not appear to cause any problems between the dogs. The peace and harmony lasted until around Niamh's 3rd year. There was a little pushing of Bronte by Niamh at times, but it seemed harmless enough. Niamh would occasionally take toys off Bronte, who would just walk away. Niamh did display a tendency to resource guard with the other dogs, but we were careful to avoid situations that might cause conflict. In March 2020 we had an incident between Niamh and Bronte. Niamh attacked and grabbed Bronte as the dogs were exiting the back door. There was no injury, as although Niamh held Bronte's scruff and shook her, she did inhibit her bite. After two further similar incidents over a few days, I sought help from Diane Garrod. The situation had quickly escalated to a serious problem. If Niamh could smell Bronte she would hunt after her, rushing from door to window to get at Bronte. If she caught sight of her through a door or window it would trigger an aggressive response with Niamh frantically lunging, barking, and attempting break through to Bronte. We had to keep Niamh separate from both the Labradors, as after the incidences with Bronte she started giving threatening looks toward Amica also. We covered the windows to block her view and placed a pen around the back door to create a safety zone. This kept the situational manageable but was by no means a solution.

Diane introduced me to the ATA (acclimate, tolerate, and accept) and we started working with Niamh and Bronte. Diane also felt that taking Niamh through the CED (Canine Emotional Detox) program would offer additional *help by addressing Niamh's anxiety and relieving the underlying stress. So, we introduced the CED early in the process. It was an intense three days, but well worth the effort. Apart from the clear benefits to Niamh, there were educational benefits for me, which would be advantageous in long term maintenance. As part of the CED Diane introduced me to Tellington TTouch and emphasized the importance of sensory activities as part of Niamh's daily routine. Niamh took to these with great pleasure. The CED also made me aware of the need to include activities, such as scent games, foraging and problem solving, on a regular basis. We introduced puzzle toys, food hunts and a snuffle mat as part of the dog's daily feeding regime. The CED also taught me how to use warmth and a quiet relaxing environment to help Niamh achieve the much-needed REM sleep. The final analysis gave a clear and detailed picture of what Niamh needed in the long term to foster a calmer more manageable dog.*

Almost a year after the initial incident we once again have peace in our household. All three dogs live in harmony and Niamh and Bronte appear to have a better relationship than they had prior to the emergence of the problem between them. They play and rest together, seemingly enjoying each other's company. We are still cautious in high arousal situations, but with careful management we feel confident we can avoid any deterioration in the relationship between the dogs or a recurrence of the problems experienced. We are very grateful for the help and guidance Diane afforded us and

the ultimate positive outcome she helped us achieve." **Pauline Dickerson,**
ARATAH DOG TRAINING, Australia

*"Quinn continues to improve since finishing his first CED . I love the
program not only what it does for dogs but also for pet guardians. The insight
it gives us is incredible. I am much more mindful now of how stress chemicals
build up in us all and how that can make it virtually impossible for us to not
react – as much as it is impossible for a boiling kettle not to let off steam. This
gives me a much better understanding of how to support and understand
Quinn's behavior. From a chihuahua who would take off over a large expanse
to do that horrid bark and nip at other dogs, we now have no trouble being
out and about where other dogs are present. In fact Quinn is a regular demo
dog for K9 Nose Work at fairs and different dog events. To have him be able
to work happily and confidently when he is surrounded by sometimes hundreds of other dogs is mind blowing. It only goes to show what we can do for
these animals when we know what to do. Diane's work is pivotal in making so
many dogs and pet guardians life better. Quinn and I are lucky to be amongst
them."* **Peta Clarke, Australia**

The CED combines several key ingredients in a unique way to help
reactive dogs feel safe and to help them overcome the fear and anxiety that
drives much of their problem behavior. It is grounded in scientific dog
training and behavior principles, including physical well-being, nutrition,

calming touch, physical stimulation, mental stimulation, and play. It is based on Applied Behavior Analysis principles.

Forward

by Ira Vaculik, Canine Behavior Counselor, Germany, www.dogopedia.de

Before

After

Lobo was one of around 2500 inhabitants of a huge Public Shelter (PS) in the far North-East of Romania, close to the Ukrainian border. Animal welfare is not a big concern in this European, but poor country, and standards are still pretty low these days. Nevertheless, street dogs were accepted by people to a certain degree until there was a tragic incident in 2013 when some of them were accused of killing a child. Due to public outrage, there was a downright chivvy (persistent petty attacks) on street dogs and thousands were killed or left to die in huge PSs with no or very little food, shelter, and care.

Nobody can tell how and for how long Lobo had to live in this PS in the North-East. It happened that I saw him in the background of a photograph one day and he looked directly into my heart. I knew I needed to find him and try to get him out of those conditions. It took me several months to locate the right contact person and eventually Lobo himself in this big country, but finally succeeded. I was very thankful and excited when my wonderful Romanian friends took him out of the miserable conditions in the PS and housed him in a private shelter to prepare him for his great journey. It was Christmas Eve of 2015.

He was said to be around 5 years old, 64 cm (25 inches)/28 kg (62 lbs.). In the following months I was told that he was "ok with dogs but very, very scared and aggressive towards people". He would not accept to be touched and had to be caught, conquered, and restrained by several people for medical care (which was mandatory due to export regulations).

In March 2016 he arrived in Germany in a cage. Nobody dared to touch him. On our trip home I never saw a hair of him in his kennel, not one sign of curiosity or interest. He was scared and totally exhausted. When I sang to him for a while he briefly lifted his head, and I could see his beautiful deep eyes in the dark for the very first time.

At home I left him with his kennel as a retreat in a separate room which I had prepared to give him quiet and recovery. Except a harm (an injury) on one forepaw he was in rather good shape physically, matted, skinny and muscle atrophied, but healthy superficially. Not something I could say about his psyche.

He was deeply traumatized, scared to death, in survival mode and highly stressed ALL THE TIME. He appeared to be feral with little to no human contact, except the one in the shelter which was not positive for sure. He barely left his crate and decided not to leave this room deliberately for weeks, and I mean weeks. At first, he came out of his crate only for food, water and to release himself on puppy pads, or at night. I couldn't touch him, which I didn't try so as not to stress him more. If I were coming closer, he would freeze, pressing against the ground and deeply growl.

He certainly would have bitten if harassed. He was fine with my other dogs but not interested. Just seeing me somewhere in the house had him totally shut down. He was lying in his bed for 24 hours a day, totally passive but with a permanent respiratory rate of over 100 bpm, pure chronic stress.

As a Dog Trainer and Behavior Counselor I specialize in behavior problems and my heart belongs especially to the fearful and deprived individuals, who (and their dedicated guardians) could benefit tremendously from a tailored destress and behavior modification program. I had many years of experience and wonderful successes with this kind of dog many client dogs and two of my own.

But I knew in this case I wanted a, very structured approach, and a bunch of new ideas. It was a great opportunity to learn more about Diane's CED which I came across some time before. I was sure Lobo and I could profit a lot from that concept. Working as a force free trainer for many years I was also sure Diane's program would meet my own benevolent philosophy and reward-based training style.

Due to his heavy burden Lobo and I went through two CED's with an interval of 6 weeks. The CED has taught me a lot about Lobo's personality, which was tough to detect as he was so shut down. It's thoughtful approach helped me to create further plans considering his shy, soft, reserved personality. I got an overall better impression of his needs and learned that he needs time to think things through and that I need even more time and smaller steps to get him out of his shell and make him progress. Diane guided me through the process with a lot of passion, knowledge and heart. Her analyses were on point and I had no clue how she managed that from far away even over the big pond. As professionals are just as much loving owners as anybody else, her comments and empathy with Lobo had me made tears come to my eyes a few times.

The systematic stress release protocol for challenging dogs will give trainers a holistic, need-oriented and force free approach to help dogs to learn problem solving skills, to gain trust in themselves and their humans, and find quality of life again. Psyche can come to peace and quiet again, and for Lobo's and my mutual path a great asset.

As I am writing these 1.5 years have passed. Our journey went on beautifully, albeit the inescapable ups and downs. A few weeks after the second CED Lobo allowed me to touch him for the first time. We grew together and share a strong and trustful bond now. He learned to accept collar and leash, which was, after supposedly caught by loop, a great challenge, and huge step for this boy. Around a year after the CEDs he made the so far biggest step and voluntarily left the house to conquer our large yard. You should have seen his expression, he felt so happy and free!

He is now part of the two- and four-legged family and apparently enjoys his new life. He found a close friend with my other Romanian rescue Lion (seen in photo above), who helped me to gain Lobo's trust from the beginning. These two are too adorable to watch. Lobo still has "moments" of evasion and retreat but doesn't last in his comfort zone for long before he seeks our company again. He is as normal as he can be after the rough life he had lived before his journey guided him to us.

By now Lobo's case is known all over the place and is even covered in relevant German literature. I hope that my experiences with this special dog and the great opportunities the CED gave us can help others. It has helped me also, with my own progress and development as a trainer of challenging dogs. Give them quiet, time and a holistic, sophisticated approach and you will all find peace and happiness. The CED was an imminent part of our progress.

Chapter 1

Internal and external discovery of the challenging canine

"Ruin and recovering are both from within."
- Epictetus, a Greek sage, and stoic philosopher

The Canine Emotional Detox (CED) is the transformation of challenging dogs through the neutralization of harmful stress chemicals. Chances are you are reading this book because you are having some challenges with your own dog or working with clients who have come to the end of their rope because their dog exhibits distressing behaviors.

The stress release protocol is on average a three-day intensive biochemical and emotional rebalancing of your dog. It must be noted that chronically stressed individuals, approximately 10% of dogs, may require additional time to de-stress. While the detox has not been the subject of formal study, anecdotally it is showing a more than 90% improvement rate of behavior problems. The participating dog's problem behavior information is gathered both before and after the stress protocol and the vast majority of cases report lasting improvement.

The CED is not a miracle cure, but it is a systematic protocol and first of its kind, which allows you to gain improvements in behavior which are sometimes rapid and surprising. When you begin to understand what happens in the dog's body to create behavioral challenges, then you begin to understand how to reach, change and satiate that individual dog to retain outward changes.

The Canine Emotional Detox (CED for short, and will be used from this point onward) is basically a stress vacation for the behaviorally troubled or challenging modern dog. The CED addresses the dog's issues by working with the inner dog or from addressing the issues from the inside out. It precedes behavior modification and skill's applications and provides a final analysis to enhance a behavior modification program and skills process. Often, as trainers we jump right into behavior modification or start listing the skill deficits, but there is a lot to consider helping that behavior modification program be more effective.

Stress can be the cause of many behavior problems and health issues. Throughout the book illustrations will be presented for ease of understanding how to transform the challenging dog through the process of the CED.

Elements of stress release

The CED helps to transform the dog through systematic stress relief, to include mentally tiring activity (sensory activities, toys, brain games and problem solving) and physical stimulation (Ttouch, massage, slow, focused obstacle courses) anything that relaxes the body. Physical exercise is allowed only if exercise is not stressful for the dog.

Stress causes dogs to go on autopilot, they are just "cruising" through life in continual reactivity or aggression. The dog is on information overload and this takes a toll on other pets and human family members in the household who become "secondary".

If you are reading this book, you know your dog is stressed, a client dog is stressed and results to start to change emotional responses means releasing stress first. Releasing the bad stress build-up equals a readiness of the dog to relax, be responsive, focus, calm, to learn and gain confidence. When bad stress (distress or acute stress, or chronic stress) neutralizes, dogs learn better, retain more, and achieve longer lasting results, as seen in hundreds of recorded cases for this edition one of the CED.

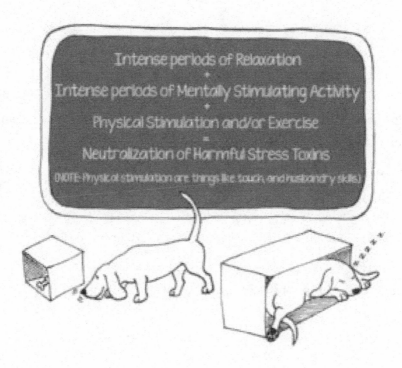

This illustration explaining the CED protocol. *Illustration by Carol Byrnes, Author of "What is my dog saying"; "What is my dog saying at the dog park" and "What is my cat saying" interactive PowerPoint CDs, available at www.dogwise.com. Carol is owner of Diamonds in the Ruff, Spokane, Washington State*

Key Concepts

The secret to the effectiveness of the CED is when the exact combinations of this illustration are done in a specific order. The order is what maximizes the release of harmful stress chemicals built-up in the brain and body. It is this right combination of events over an intense 72 -hour period that releases stress and builds eustress, the good stress chemicals, so a dog can learn, be calm and focused. (See Chapter Five, titled "The Right Combination").

The CED journey begins with having a challenging canine, whether that means aggression, high-level reactivity (dog to dog, multi-dog family fighting; dog human; environmental sensitivities), hyperactivity, separation anxiety, over-excitement or stimulation, OCD (obsessive compulsive disorders), PTSD (post traumatic stress syndrome), fear or any combination of these behaviors.

What came first the chicken or the egg, the CED or my research? The journey had to start with the CED before my research was applied to explaining why it was working to release stress, or the time came to ask, why is this working? In asking why, I chose a certain approach.

It was evident I was asking a question about a natural phenomenon, stress. So in looking deeper there were five elements that begged for research:

- **Stress and the canine** – Why and how does stress affect thinking and sleep in challenging canines?

- **Making observations** of the phenomenon case by case had to be a part of the process.

- **Real life cases** (Citizen Science) were chosen and identifying patterns became the foundation.

- **Hypothesizing an explanation** for the phenomenon and the resulting discovery, that behavior modification programs weren't always effective in releasing canine stress. Behavior modification was taking longer or coming to a standstill.

- **Predicting a logical consequence of the hypothesis** became a need to understand why the neutralization of the bad chemicals in brain and body meant the canine learns better, faster and retains longer during and after a CED. This was exactly the reality being seen in CED after CED.

Five elements were chosen in testing the hypothesis:

Definition of a hypothesis: A hypothesis is a tentative statement about the natural world leading to deductions that can be tested. If the deductions are verified, it becomes more probable that the hypothesis is correct. If the deductions are incorrect, the original hypothesis can be abandoned or modified. Hypotheses can be used to build more complex inferences and explanations. **National Academy of Sciences**

- a large sample size; a long period of time; a control group of permission-based studies
- using real clients
- using real trainers
- using very challenging canines, in various environments , with many different behaviors
- plus follow through and follow up POST detox with clients
- Creating a conclusion with data gathered was the final step for edition one of this book.

Behavior change using the CED

The canine emotional detox used before a behavior modification program or skills training process creates a canine who is ready to think, is able to focus, learns concepts faster, and retains information longer.

A question I am asked is "Does it have to be three full days?" The answer to that question is a resounding yes, three fully dedicated days to the process of stress neutralization as it takes 72-hours (Brown, Ali, M.Ed., CPDT, "Scaredy Dog!" 2004) for the body to come down from stress chemicals that have built up internally in the body and brain, providing the dog is in good health and not chronically stressed, according to Mayo Clinic, Constant Stress Puts Your Heart at Risk. It is a process. Dogs who are in chronic stress, or continually stressed and unable to come down naturally, may take longer. Longer means a second CED, one month after the first, or longer, as in consecutive days five to 21. On average, dogs will respond to three full days of the CED stress-release protocol (as indicated in the over 700 permission-based cases researched in this process).

To understand how and why the CED works it is important to look at a brief overview of what the CED is, and again, the order in which the CED is done, to understand why it is effective. There are many articles, books, studies on stress in dogs and how to help the dog to release stress leaving it up to the reader to implement the how to (see RESOURCES at end of this book for further reading). The CED provides an order to stress release, a step-by-step process and looks at the canine from the inside outwardly.

What makes the CED unique?

First and foremost, it is force free, meaning non-confrontational, using desensitization and counter conditioning. It is a systematic process to get to a state of deep REM (rapid eye movement) sleep. The CED neutralizes harmful stress chemicals and replaces with feel good chemicals helping a dog on an anxiety medication to utilize that medication better or to forego medication altogether.

Further, the CED presents an option to precede a behavior modification or skills program so those are more successful or it has the versatility to complement an in-process program. It allows the dog to use cognitive abilities so sustained learning can take place. It strengthens relationships, bonds between dog and pet guardian and gives trainer an insider view of pet guardian, family and dog's environment that goes beyond an intake form or functional analysis allowing a very real snapshot at what life is like with this individual dog. The end process is a dog that learns better, faster and retains longer for lasting results. It speeds the behavior modification process because stress has been reduced.

When a stress release process is outlined, most behavior consultants/ trainers will suggest increasing exercise or simply start right out with a behavior modification or skill's applications process after a functional analysis. The truth is the dog may not be ready to learn or to handle that process.

Some training plans for challenging dogs may call for relaxation only for a few consecutive days or until the dog relaxes fully and the result is release of harmful stress chemicals. This could take weeks or months.

Some plans call for increasing exercise. In an all exercise-based program if increased exercise is stressful for the dog, then the exercise in and of itself can be stressful because triggers and stimuli are present and causing distress. If exercise is enjoyed and non-reactive, then it does, in fact, effectively release glucocorticoids, according to Brown, Ali, M.Ed., CPDT, "Scaredy Dog!" 2004. Exercise can be a powerful addition to a stress release process. While exercise and relaxation are needed in a results- oriented process to release stress, it is the combination done in the right order that is the key to success.

Let's talk about glucocorticoids – what are they?

Glucocorticoids are steroid or stress hormones produced by the adrenal cortex. The word pertains to glucose + cortex. Cortisol (hydrocortisone) is one of the most important glucocorticoids. Cortisol is essential for life, yet too much cortisol or too little have detrimental health effects on the system.

What do glucocorticoids have to do with stress and learning?

An empirical relationship between arousal and performance was originally developed by psychologists Robert M. Yerkes and John Dillingham Dodson in 1908 and named the Yerkes Dodson Law. The law dictates that performance increases with physiological or mental arousal, but only up to a point. When levels of arousal become too high, performance decreases. In relation to glucocorticoids, a 2007 review by Lupien SJ, Maheu F, Tu M, Fiocco A, and Schramek TE (2007) of the effects of stress hormones (glucocorticoids, GC) revealed that for a situation to induce a stress response, it has to be interpreted as novel, and/or unpredictable, and/or not controllable by the individual, and/or a social evaluative threat (negative social evaluation possibly leading to social rejection).

Glucocorticoids act on the hippocampus, amygdala, and frontal lobes (Cahill L, McGaugh JL (July 1998). In multiple animal studies, prolonged stress (causing prolonged increases in glucocorticoid levels) have shown destruction of the neurons in this area of the brain, which has been connected to memory performance. Excessive glucocorticoids are not good for animal or human systems.

Loss or profound diminishment of glucocorticoid secretion leads to a state of deranged metabolism and an inability to deal with stressors. Several aspects of cognitive function are known to both stimulate glucocorticoid secretion and be influenced by glucocorticoids. Fear-inducing stimuli lead to secretion of glucocorticoids from the adrenal gland, and treatment of phobic individuals with glucocorticoids prior to a fear-inducing stimulus can blunt the fear response. "Virtually any type of physical or mental stress results in elevation of cortisol concentrations in blood due to enhanced secretion of CRH in the hypothalamus. This fact sometimes makes it difficult to assess glucocorticoid levels, particularly in animals, as being restrained for blood sampling is enough stress to artificially elevate cortisol levels several fold," according to Bowen, R. May 2006, Colorado State, "Glucocorticoids".

Which canines will benefit most from a CED?

Dogs who will benefit greatly from the stress neutralizing effects of the CED are those that:

- repeat over-the-top behaviors (such as licking, or obsessive behaviors 'OCD')
- have bite histories (aggressive displays and high-level reactivity)
- exhibit constant barking
- have a high-level anxiety and stress
- have dog to dog reactions or aggression issues

- are in a multi-dog family and fighting
- have various levels of reactivity (reactions to scary objects, sounds, humans or dogs)
- suffer from separation anxiety (SA)
- have post-traumatic stress syndrome (PTSD)
- are fearful, feral or both

Other canines that will benefit from a CED are senior dogs with health issues and hyperactive or highly-stressed adolescents. A CED is also productive for board and train programs, shelter, and foster dogs, dogs who will soon have a new puppy or baby added to a household, and dogs who make a transitional move of any type.

The CED, done correctly, is designed to work with the canine from the inside outwardly to release stress, anxiety, and tension. It can and has, in hundreds of permission-based and researched cases, shortened the rehabilitation time and has definite positive, results-oriented effects when a behavior modification program and skills process are added. These case studies were done in an applied behavior approach where the majority were implemented by the dog pet guardian/pet guardian in a real life, real home environment, shelter, or foster experience. Several cases will be referred to throughout this book.

What dog age groups were represented?

Puppies were such a miniscule sampling; they are not even worth mentioning. Puppies can definitely be stressed for a variety of reasons, but often pet guardians believe they will grow out of their behaviors and do not call until the behavior has become habituated or out-of-hand. They represented smallest age group.

Behavior issues started appearing in adolescence, and over 18M to four years making up second largest group, not far behind adult dogs aged four and over.

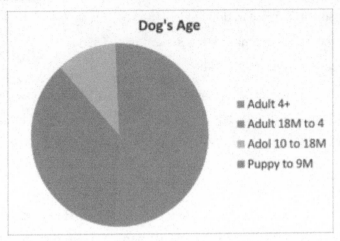

Navie and Soho's Story: Two female littermates, fighting, adolescents aged 1 year 5 months

The behavior was described as general anxiety, separation anxiety, constant arousal, fighting with each other. When the dogs arrived for board and train, the trainer saw some disturbing behavior.

"They both literally moved their crates snarling, lunging, and growling teeth bared at me just for walking by to shut the light off." -Whitney W,, trainer, Canada

Before *the CED, implemented by a trainer in Canada in a board and train, Soho above, was fighting with another female, Navie, in a four-dog household. As you can see, Soho was extremely fearful, worried and in avoidance.*

Above, **is day two** *of the CED. Soho is wearing a Thundershirt (www. thundershirt.com) and is a bit more confident, rested, calmer and curious although she is in a different environment.*

The rest of Navie and Soho's Story

Before, *above, Navie day one fearful and stuck to back of crate.*

Above, day two, *happier. What happens internally when a dog becomes stressed, versus what the CED does to allow the ability for the dog to become more confident.*

It is important to understand why the CED works. Understanding is knowing what is happening and how to make lasting changes in behavior. Often a dog pet guardian, trainer may have tried many things or say they've tried *everything* and yet the canine still shows signs of distress and unreliability and is probably the reason you are reading this book. The CED helps to nail down exactly what is happening with the distressed dog, making what is done next with technique, modification, skills more effective and longer lasting.

Today, the two dogs Soho and Navie are working a behavior modification process for multi-dog households fighting. In the photo above, they can even take food close to each other without fighting.

Many other multi-dog households fighting, like Navi and Soho, have had successful CEDs followed by a step-by-step behavior modification process of acclimation, tolerance and acceptance.

In the beginning of the CED, based on where each individual is in their learning, limited treats are used, and touch or clicker training may or may not yet be a part of the process. Often challenging dogs are too stressed to eat, to play, to be touched and loud sounds are not positive for them. Each dog is unique and the CED is customized for maximum effectiveness.

How to determine a CED is successful

There will be a noticeable release or neutralization of bad stress, and a noticeable change in the dog's whole body as muscles relax. Photos of dogs before and after reveal amazing changes in body tension.

Photos below are of Gabriel, Doberman Pinscher, **before and after** CED (see his story in Chapter 3). Gabriel's CED was done as a part of his board and train process and lasted eight days out of a 14-day stay. He was one of the first CED real life cases, and his behavior modification had hit a wall. During the CED, eventually he was able to relax, to release muscle tension, and to diminish constant barking. It took five days to see results in barking, and the next three days body tension released, and achievement of deep sleep completed the cycle.

Before

After

Very tight, always on alert, unable to relax and wearing a head halter, all exchanged for a happier, more responsive, more confident dog able to relax and no longer needing head collar.

"To the untrained eye, your dog may appear to be in a state of calm acceptance. Misused equipment, intimidation or restraint may cause a condition called tonic immobility, wherein fear is mistaken and mislabeled as "good behavior". Tonic immobility is a condition of unresponsiveness occurring during significant stress. Tonic immobility may occur at a training facility, lesson or class, at home, or in any situation where a pet is frightened" (Michaels, 2021, in Flooding and Tonic Immobility). Michaels, L.J. (2021). Do no harm dog training and behavior: Featuring the Hierarchy of Dog Needs. "Do No Harm" Dog Training Manual Author https://gumroad.com/l/ trainingmanual , Rated One of the Top Ten U.S. Dog Trainers

There will be a noticeable change in the way a dog feels internally and a noticeable change in the way a dog feels emotionally and physically. The CED will have provided visual deep, heavy NREM (non-REM) and REM sleep patterns. A dog's problem-solving profile will have been completed through mentally tiring activities and subtle shifts in brain chemistry will alter behavior, noticeably. Mood, concentration (focus), memory (sustainable learning to make good decisions) will all be altered. The CED will have a lasting effect of up to two months. Effect will be longer if a behavior modification process is put into place. A noticeable renewal of the dog, pet guardian relationship and bond will surface. The CED provides revelations as to how the dog handles real life making it easier and more effective to implement a behavior modification program and assess skills applications.

CHAPTER 2

The Paw on the Writer's Hand

Belgian Tervuren, Chancellor

In memory of and thanks to Chancellor my muse. April 3, 2004 to January 24, 2015. Without him this book would not have been written.

Never apologize for showing feeling, compassion, empathy for your dog. When you do so, you apologize for the truth behind creating a positive relationship. – Diane Garrod, Author The Canine Emotional Detox: Stress Release for the Challenging Dog

It would not be a complete process if the inspiration for the CED were not revealed. The actual CED started with 50 pre-cases in the exploration of feasibility (not permission-based) and evolved into over 700 further cases, permission based. Permission-based meaning I can talk about these cases because the dog pet guardians signed a permission release form.

The research started with my own dog Chancellor, who had over-the-top behaviors, a genetic component resulting in a very human reactive, and neurologically challenged canine. My own dog, work partner, best friend, Chancellor has made me laugh and made me cry. He is the inspiration urging the muse in me to write, to study, to develop and to create the CED.

Chancellor is the pen, the keyboard, the creator in a way only a true teacher dog could be. He is as much a part of the process as are all the other and continuing recorded cases.

Chancellor's Story

The changes were nothing short of systematically remarkable, despite Chancellor's genetic health and temperament issues, genetic factors in the breed, and in the litter, as I would come to find out later. Systematic CC & DS (Counter Conditioning and Desensitization) and even Tellington Touch was not getting results for Chancellor who was highly reactive toward humans.

Two people, Kathy Cascade a physical therapist and Tellington Touch Instructor, and Jennifer White, Laughing Dog and i2iK9 would be the influences to get me started and thinking about approaches to Chancellor's behavior taking me out of my comfort zone to all previously learned solutions. They were also instrumental in showing me that what I was doing was on the right path.

From the time I brought him home, at 9 weeks, he promptly snapped at the veterinarian on his first check-up on the way home. Chancellor's human reactivity got worse and by ten months old he reacted to a conformation instructor in class. By 14-months-old he had a similar reaction to an AKC ring judge, it became apparent Chancellor would not go on to perform in the show ring despite his good structure and a co-pet guardianship agreement with the breeder.

With people interactions, it didn't matter who or why, nor that he would meet them and then would have to start over. Even if he had met them before it did not mean he would welcome them back. His behavior would escalate and he would complete a sequence of freeze, growl, bark, snarl, air snap and back away.

He would also do this to me or a caretaker he really liked if his space perimeter were violated. He had never, to my knowledge, been hurt before he came to live with us at nine-weeks-old. When I went to pick Chancellor (Wyld Waves of Chance) up from the breeders I saw a puppy less than eager to come to the stranger (me) and slinking along the baseboards. He was the puppy who stayed to the back of the exercise pen while several others came forward. From day one I knew he would be a challenge, but I am a force free trainer, I could handle it. The journey we would take would truly be Wyld Waves of Chance (Chancellor's AKC registered name).

Chancellor was trained using force free methods from the beginning, and it was a good thing and that which would later make a huge difference in his steady and progressive transformation. Still in dealing with his behavior and at the end of my knowledge I turned to others. Those others recommended sending him back to the breeder, or taking him to an academy known for the use of prong, choke and shock collars to "fix him", "whip him into shape." The final straw was a medical professional that had the additional nerve to tell me to alpha roll him and said, "maybe that is what he needs." In hindsight, any aversive technique would have ruined this dog and he probably would not have lived to almost 11-years-old (4/03/2004 to 1/24/2015).

While desperate people do desperate things, and I was desperate, as well as doubting my knowledge as a trainer, it was at the urgings of an online friend that Chancellor (then 4-months-old) and I head, instead of to an aversive academy, to Tellington Touch training. Just the thought of being in a class situation, in an environment with multiple people, and lots of distractions, was enough to make me nervous and could be enough to send Chancellor over-threshold when least expected. Although he was able to relax, as soon as it became evident people were moving around, talking, staring at him, he would be visibly distressed and growl, bark, lunge, air snap and back up. I had to constantly be assertive and remind people not to reach out, not to squat down, not to approach the exercise pen and not to pet him.

Little progress was made with Chancellor during Ttouch trainings, that came later. While I started Ttouch training because of Chancellor, I finished my Tellington Touch practitioner certification despite Chancellor. It was clear this would be a great tool for me and help many other client dogs in the process. Ultimately, Ttouch became important in my work with Chancellor too. The CED started to grow, to birth and to move into the toddler stage, and then to blossom, as I continued to struggle with and deal with my dog's behavior issues. Like many guardians, I thought Chancellor would grow out of it, we would work through it, maybe I did something wrong, or this is how Belgian Tervurens were as pups.

As I started to learn more, focus on behavior, I started re-analyzing Chancellor's behavior and from his age of four-month-olds onward, my gut kept shouting at me that Chancellor's challenges were not only behavioral, but the behavior was because of something neurological. It was out of my control to change, to stop and genetically, health-wise, it would have to reveal its ugly head when it was ready. In the meantime, eye rolls could not even start to describe the looks and responses I would get if I even dared to bring this point up. So, I kept it to myself and continued to study and observe. I was determined that if there was nothing out there to help my dog that I would create something to help him that stayed completely within the guidelines of force free, results-oriented, and science-based methodology according to applied behavior analysis. I did not realize that in the process I would also be developing a schematic for challenging dogs of all types.

The future tumbled forward and as Chancellor turned 4.5 years old on September 19, 2008, at 9:25 a.m., he fell to the floor in the midst of playing with my other Belgian Tervuren, Kody Bear, of the same age. He thrashed, lost control of urine and to me seemingly lost consciousness. I did not know what to do, I had never experienced this and I was scared to death. I thought Chancellor was dying. Chancellor was having his first grand mal seizure. This dog I had come to love, to bond deeply with, to have behavioral progress, to have a relationship bar none, was helpless before me and needed me now more than ever. The neurological issue had reared its ugly head.

Nothing could have prepared me for the brutality of a first seizure or that day and that moment and yet it opened wide the door to what the Canine Emotional Detox (CED) is today, a systematic stress neutralization process for challenging dogs. It forced me to transform Chancellor's challenges while transforming his health issues.

Stress can cause a seizure, i.e., the stress of company, the stress of me being away, the stress of meeting new people and so on. It forced me to look deeply at what we are doing to dogs in society and it forced me to take a closer, deeper look at my client dogs. Chancellor's behavioral issues, genetic issues, health issues transferred seamlessly into other areas of my training challenging dogs to include board and train, private clients, shelter and foster dogs, dogs with health issues current or pending and of course, to my own dogs. It was a moment of realization that there is a whole puzzle to solving challenging behaviors over and above just jumping right into the behavior modification process or skills applications. Without all the pieces, without the missing link to stress release in challenging dogs, it would be like jumping out of a plane without a parachute.

The CED and Chancellor

Chancellor needed more than Tellington Touch, more than behavior modification, more than skills applications, although all those pieces would be ultimately important to his change. Chancellor was an untouchable dog. It did not feel good to him, he did not welcome it from me or anyone else. He needed stress relief to cope with real life. Stress exacerbates health issues, seizures, and manifests itself in perceived danger scenarios, whether there is or is not cause. Perceived threat is enough to cause stress, according to Primary Headship newsletter. Health issues can cause perceived threat.

To neutralize Chancellor's daily exposure to stress, I began to design a system he could live with and that would also transform his behavioral issues, and that system started from the moment he woke up, until the moment he went to bed at night. How he started his day made a huge difference in the rest of the day and the coping skills he used. The CED was born. Chancellor changed. A former client said to me, *"The day I met Chancellor, I just couldn't believe he had had any issues at all." Connie O'Hara, retired breeder, trainer, Useless Bay, WA.* She met him in a room filled with people during a Kathy Cascade S.A.N.E. Solutions seminar, walking around off lead, touching people with his nose, and getting rewards.

On January 24, 2015 at 6:38 a.m., Chancellor passed away peacefully and naturally in my arms, in his own home surrounded by those he loved and who loved him deeply surrounded by his things. In our hallway he started his life with us, he had his first seizure there and he passed away in that hallway. His job, his purpose on earth was done. RIP my dear friend, I know many will benefit from your journey.

Chapter 3

How to tell if a dog is stressed and its severity

Stress is a nonspecific response of the body when any demand is placed upon it. Any biological or psychological demand will result in stress. The demand does not necessarily have to involve an aversive stimulation for stress to occur. Mild stress can improve learning and provide beneficial mental and physical stimulation. Excessive stress leads to distress. James O'Heare glossary definition, "Aggressive Behavior in Dogs"" 2007 General Adaptation Syndrome and contrast with Distress

What are the beneficial components of stress release?

The CED has these beneficial components:

- allows for neutralization of stress
- dog begins to learn and process information better
- works with the senses of smell (olfactory), taste, hearing (auditory), vision
- uses mentally tiring activities to create new ways of thinking and feeling all of which will be a part of a results-oriented, positive, force free, reward-based learning system
- transforms the dog from the inside outwardly
- changes the dog's body language from tense to calm
- initiates deep, undisturbed sleep.
- releases stress so a dog can go through the behavior modification procedure, think better, quicker and retain longer.

Hans Selye, considered by many as the father of the study of stress, developed the idea that a direct relationship exists between chronic stress and excessive wear and tear throughout the body.

What is occurring in the dog's body is important to understanding why the CED is effective in stress release. Stress might be looked at as the equivalent to human burn out. Stress can cause a dog to be more likely to react or aggress and to exhibit a few other behaviors, such as licking, over-barking, hyperactivity and more. Stress in dogs is a reality trainers face working with highly challenging dogs.

Challenging dogs are defined as those who are distressed, or acutely stressed or chronically stressed. These are the dog reactive dogs and the dog human reactive dogs, as well as the environmentally sensitive dogs, the multi-dog households fighting, fear aggressive dogs and those showing any reactive or aggressive behaviors. Stress affects senior dogs, dogs who are ill, and those experiencing changes such as moving to a new home, being relinquished to a shelter, a death in the family, or a divorce.

It is important to understand that stress is a needed life function. It protects, but stress that is constant, levels out and becomes a part of every-day life is not normal. It can become acute and chronic.

This book will talk about distress, acute stress, and chronic stress. The differing levels of stress are defined as follows:

Mild cases

Immediate effects of stress or low level (distress)

The immediate effects of stress activate the sympathetic nervous system (SNS) and release epinephrine and norepinephrine. The release happens quickly within two to three seconds, like a blink of an eye. The dog can come down from distress quickly.

Moderate cases

Intermediate effects of stress or high level (acute stress)

The intermediate effects cause an adrenal response where epinephrine and norepinephrine are also released but from the adrenal medulla. It takes about 20 to 30 seconds to spike, like warming up a coffee in the microwave. The spikes are higher, but the dog can still come down from the stress.

The CED will work wonders on distress/acute stress and into normal ranges while building eustress, the mood enhancing stress or good stress.

Severe or extreme cases

Prolonged effects of stress or extreme level (chronic stress). Stress has leveled out, become chronic (continuous), the dog is like one with an addiction, constantly stressed. This type of prolonged stress affects various metabolic processes such as adrenocorticotropic hormone (ACTH), a hormone released from the pituitary gland in the brain, vasopressin (a hormone secreted by cells of the hypothalamic nuclei), and thyroxine affecting various metabolic processes. This can cause various health issues to occur. Chronic stress lingers minutes, hours, days, weeks, months, like a cancer. It takes longer to get rid of, but occurs in only 10% of tested cases.

Constant stress creates a chemical bath to the brain and body of bad stress chemicals adrenalin, cortisol, neoepinephrine, and noradrenaline versus good chemicals or mood enhancers of oxytocin, endorphins, dopamine, and serotonin.

Gabriel's Story – Extreme Case – Doberman Pinscher, Bellingham, Washington State

What a dog feels internally is what causes things to happen externally
- Pavlov

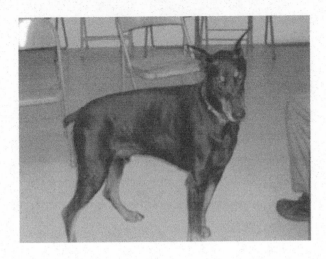

Gabriel was dog reactive, human reactive, environmentally sensitive, over-barking and edgy all the time. He was loved by his family, but they did not know how to help him. What was noticeable in Gabriel's case is the fact behavior modification was done first, 15 weeks and some progress was made. With the intensity of his dog reactivity (after being attacked by a few dogs before we began working, and in addition being sent to a boot camp type training situation) the goal was to be able to walk past other dogs without incident. This goal was reached, but Gabriel remained stressed, over-barked and could not be trusted. We were able to work through his human reactivity and interaction with the grandkids. The turning point came when his guardians took a trip to Hawaii and Gabriel boarded with me, Caninetlc B&B, for 14 days. The first eight days were an intense CED, with the first five days continuous barking. After five days, you could hear a pin drop, the quiet very noticeable. He was a different dog from that point on. Gabriel lived the rest of his days with his guardians and passed on due to cancer a few years ago. Noticeable body changes occur when stress and tension release. Often the dog looks like a different dog .

The CED is a much-needed stress vacation for dogs, but in a structured, systematic protocol within the physiology, biologics, cognition, and deep REM sleep focuses.

DEFINITION of stress is the lack of fit between the perceived demands of the environment and the perceived ability to cope with those demands.

According to "The Primary Headship" Apr 2007, a teaching expertise newsletter, "stress occurs in dogs as well as in humans and is described as the epidemic of the 21st Century. Stress causes dogs to go on auto pilot, they are just "cruising" through life in continual reactivity or aggression becoming end result. The dog is on information overload and this takes a toll on other pets in the household who become secondary."

A sentence from James O'Heare's book, Aggressive Behavior in Dogs, describes it perfectly, *"In order for behavior change procedures to influence what the dog learns, the dog's level of stress must be reduced."*

The stress release protocol provides a deeper understanding of distress and how it affects learning and behavior. Stress release is a key piece to assist challenging dogs in adjusting to a behavior modification protocol and/or a skills applications process.

Most dogs today just get up, eat, walk, return home, sleep while pet guardian goes to work and then repeat the cycle when the pet guardian comes home from work. The dog eats dinner or free feeds throughout the day, and then goes for a walk, returns home, plays a game of fetch, and sleeps, waking up several times during the night. This schedule leaves little time for the body to heal, to repair, to build serotonin or melatonin. Bad stress levels increase, good chemicals (eustress) decrease. If challenging behaviors are repeated, they level out, become habituated, and create acute or chronic stress. The result is an environment filled with stress, with boring days and nights and the start of high level reactivity and even aggression.

Starting point – Assessing stress severity – take the stress test

To assess whether a CED is needed, trainers should apply the stress test below to each individual. If one of these behaviors are seen, it will indicate a dog is distressed (a sign basically), three to five means dog may be acutely stressed and over five, dog could be chronically stressed. The difference in latter two would be that it takes more time to reduce stress if a dog is chronically stressed. Higher level behaviors could benefit from a systematic stress release protocol and a behavior modification program to more effectively change emotional responses.

- ☐ Does dog go into fight mode when their trigger/stimuli appears?
- ☐ Write down all dog's triggers and apply antecedents (what occurs prior to behavior).
- ☐ Does dog flee or try to escape when trigger/stimuli appears? Do they panic?
- ☐ Is dog overly energetic? Does dog get over-excited, over-stimulated, hyper-aroused easily?
- ☐ Is dog hyper-alert or extremely alert to the environment and cannot focus?
- ☐ Is dog refusing treats? Do you find client saying "My dog doesn't take treats" or "My dog doesn't like treats". Not taking rewards can indicate the dog is at a high level of stress, the body is in survival mode.
- ☐ Does dog become irritable and restless even though there seems to be no danger?
- ☐ Is client removing or redirecting dog many times per day?
- ☐ Does dog have a hard time sleeping through the night? Is sleep easily interrupted? When client moves, does dog move?
- ☐ Does dog pace, whine, bite or have obsessive compulsive behaviors (tail chasing, shadow chasing etc.)?
- ☐ Has dog had recent pain, stress, infection, surgery, or trauma?
- ☐ Does dog have increases in heart rate, respiration, blood pressure or metabolism that are noticeable and long-lasting?
- ☐ Is dog tense? Are muscles stiff and tight?
- ☐ Are pupils dilated?
- ☐ Does dog pant a lot when it is not hot out, nor have they been exercising? Do they sweat from the pads of their feet making paw marks on flooring?

☐ Does dog react quickly and effectively to triggers?

☐ Could dog be described as moody?

Are there issues with food? and eating? (too fast, too slow, walks away from, will not eat in presence of guardian, resource guarding)

☐ Does dog appear depressed?

☐ Is dog aggressive? (intent to do harm)

☐ Does dog have any other over-the-top behaviors?

☐ Does client make excuses for dog?

☐ Does dog have health issues?

☐ Does dog show any of the indicators below of excessive or unhealthy stress? Check all that apply:

☐ Diarrhea

☐ Vomiting

☐ Panting

☐ Excessive barking, whining

☐ Aggression

☐ Pacing

☐ Excessive licking

☐ Digging

☐ Chewing

☐ Biting the leash

☐ Shedding

☐ Dandruff

☐ Sweaty Paws

☐ Red eyes

☐ Foam drool

☐ Tense muscles

☐ Bloat

☐ Dilated pupils

☐ Excessive tail wagging

☐   Shivering (when it is not cold)

The behaviors in the list should be very noticeable and occur daily or many times weekly. If you checked two or more boxes, the dog can benefit from a Canine Emotional Detox.

Chapter 4
Stress Release Preparation Essentials

Once it is decided a dog can benefit from a CED, preparing the essentials is next. Schedule a CED with client, allowing a consecutive 72-hours (three days). In this chapter, I'll talk about the preparation essentials.

DO THIS: Send this preparation list one week prior to implementing the stress vacation protocol.

Basic Preparation Essentials – All Behaviors

Items may be added or deleted and customized to each dog's challenges. This is a general list of items you will need to begin the process. Clients should have almost everything in their home. Be creative with props, for instance, mops and brooms for cavelletti sticks in obstacle course segment.

Biologics

Biologics are taken on day one and again on day three for comparison. First thing in the morning is best. Evaluation provides insight and reference points, as well as viable recommendation to see veterinarian.

How to links provided in resource section of this book, under YouTube references.

- taking resting respiratory rate (breaths per minute – how to in resource section)
- temperature (if you have that or last reading from chart at the vet) – see how to in resource section
- weighing your dog (or last recorded weight from vet and date taken)
- waste photo
- check gums and report a) red or b) pale white c) pink
- pH urine strip (available at any pharmacy or online) – see how to in resource section

Advise client to please take digital photographs and video

Video should be short, in 30 to 1:30 packages only. The options are that client can email as they go, send a mid-day report and/or an end of day report **by 6 p.m.** their time.

DO THIS: Advise client to end day at 6 p.m. sharp. The CED is an intense, systematic process and client will be tired.

Ask client to let it be known what they did not get to in the structured day-to-day protocols. Those will go into next day's protocol. Encourage them to finish all the items, in the order written.

Client can upload video, digitals and documents to Google Drive, Dropbox or Evernote, whichever is preferred. They should invite trainer into the folder. Videos can also be uploaded to YouTube if that is easier. At the very least all materials can be sent via email, video in an mp4 format. Ask client to let you know which is their preferred method.

What client will need to have on hand:

If a client is already feeding a whole food, cooked or raw diet, then keep this diet in place throughout the CED. If a client has their dogs on medication, keep those in the schedule. If a dog is allergic to foods, or has other dietary restrictions, make sure the detoxification diet reflects this staying away from problem foods, or keep them on their current diet. If taking medication (especially if on an antibiotic) or on a specialized diet suggests adding a probiotic, prebiotic supplement, or whole yogurt. Duration of the detox diet is three days only.

Internal detox – food choices – sensory (taste) and cleansing

The CED looks and works with a dog from the inside outwardly. An internal detox is a part of that process. No kibbled food throughout the 3 days. This diet will allow the dog's system to detoxify and cleanse and lower stress levels. It allows the trainer to see how the dog is eating and processing their food. It feels good to purge any waste build-up in the intestines. It creates a sense of well-being in the dog. Portions must be suitable for weight and age. This cleansing diet is one a veterinarian would recommend to an ill dog, so it is light, easily digestible. It helps release toxin build-ups from the environment and supports body to naturally detoxify through the liver, kidneys, gut, and skin.

Suggested main meal proteins and fiber are:

One meat protein Chicken, turkey, OR halibut are preferred, and all contain small amounts of natural relaxant, tryptophan. These foods are more to satisfy, as the tryptophan (*graph on tryptophan*) contained is minimal, and meat used should be available in client's area, cooked or raw, organic, grass fed is ideal and preferable, but at a minimum package should say no antihistamines, no hormones, minimally processed. Serving sizes 1/8 to ¼ cup small breeds; ½ to 1.5 cups medium breeds; 2 to 3 cups giant breeds per meal, served two times per day.

Below is a chart from Nutrition Data to indicate where on scale meats fall as regards tryptophan levels. More important, is which foods are readily available for purchase in the locale the CED is being done?

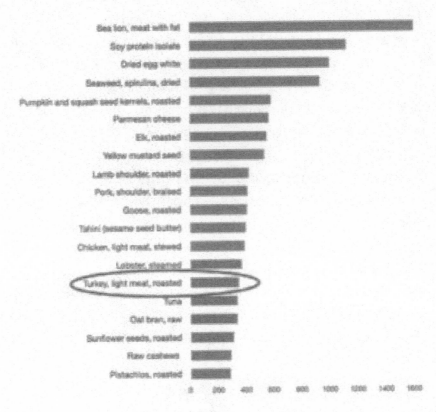

[Source Nutrition Data]

Originally, it was thought that turkey meat contains high levels of the amino acid, tryptophan. As a nutritionist explained it, once absorbed, tryptophan is used by the body to produce serotonin (a neurotransmitter) and melatonin (a hormone). The neurological pathway through which serotonin works has anti-anxiety and calming effects and melatonin help to induce feelings of drowsiness (i.e. enhances sleep). Therefore, the theory goes, after consuming a high-protein meal one that is high in tryptophan, the body's production of melatonin and serotonin increase, which in turn cause drowsiness, reduced anxiety, and a calm state of mind. It has since been proven that consuming turkey to induce drowsiness or reduce anxiety is a myth. Turkey meat does not actually contain a uniquely high level of tryptophan, as shown here in the chart.

One fiber Preference is organic canned pumpkin or fresh pumpkin, or sweet potato. Alternatives can be used, such as brown rice (more nutrient dense than white and white might spike sugar levels; both can ferment in the body), quinoa or cooked steel cut oatmeal (filled with B vitamins). Serving sizes (half of protein servings): 1/16 to 1/8 cup small breeds; ¼ to ¾ cup medium breed; 1 to 1.5 cups for giant breed per meal served two times per day.

CED day two food (only) addition to main meal Carbohydrates are added in day two and day three for energy in the form of vegetables. Carrots or sweet potatoes also provide a sensory taste of sweet. They are introduced only in day two. If using pumpkin as a main meal fiber, this addition can be skipped. Serving size will be 1/16 (small, medium dogs) to 1/8 cup (large breed). Serve warm, then process in blender or food processor or mash finely with a fork. Fresh, organic carrots are preferred.

CED day three food (only) addition to main meal Eliminate carrots and add a green for a sensory taste of sour. Pick one green vegetable. It can be broccoli, brussel sprouts, green beans or a kale, romaine lettuce, red or green lettuce. Serving size will be 1/16 (small, medium dogs) to 1/8 cup (large breed). Organic is best, serve first three cooked, or fresh lettuce and put in blender or food processor for ease of mixing into main meal.

Treats Recommending no preservatives – any protein that is part of detox diet, bits of liver, or organic dog treats, dehydrated treats, no salt, no sugar, no soy, no grains. Serving sizes 1/2 cup for daily activities. Stay away from hot dogs, cheese, peanut butter treats, tuna brownies, or treats filled with preservatives. Other tasty sensory items that may or may not be used are to proof cold tolerance. Have guardian prepare ice cubes with a berry or other fruit in the middle. This exercise will be to assess how a dog handles cold. They can be prepared in advance.

This is a detoxifying diet, suitable for three days only, as it is not sustainable nutritionally. Going back to preCED food or recommending a nutritious homemade or raw feeding schedule or consult with canine nutrition expert is postCED step. (See Chapter seven The Dog Within, The Importance of Digestion)

Relaxers

One relaxer to release tension will be a warm towel or blanket from dryer. In sunny climates, dogs can get a comparable effect by sunbathing.

Having a Thundershirt (www.thundershirt.com) on hand and/or Ace brand bandages in ½-inch size (or cut a 1-inich size in half) for small dogs, 1 "size for medium size dogs, and 2 to 3-inch size for large breed dogs are advised. The Ace brand bandages are used in Tellington Touch wraps (see resources under websites for further information).

Activity Needs

Activities will be a primary focus to mentally tiring the dog. It is important to exercise the mind and not just that body. Below is a list of items to gather for the CED. Sizes of items should be according to size of dog.

- Three plastic cups differing sizes for find it games and problem-solving. Plastic is easier to push over to get reward underneath.

- Five or six different colored plastic cups or Easter eggs for color recognition problem-solving exercise.

- Three sticks to step over as obstacle items. These sticks can be in the format of mops, booms, or 2-inch by 2-inch wood, or plastic PVC pipes.

- Cones, cups, or bottles to weave around. Chairs also work fine. Obstacle items should be those people have around the house, such as empty bottles or cans.

Most dogs have a lot of toys, but if not, buying two or three is needed. A cardboard box to put toys in or formal toy box with lid is advised. A variety of toys is advised, interactive, talking, colorful toys.

Agility obstacles, homemade is fine. These obstacles are something to go into or under, such as a tunnel, a tarp, towel, or blanket over a chair can substitute. For climbing items such as a pause table, laundry basket, a box, a couch is fine. A broom or mop handle between two chairs makes a great jump.

Three strips of cloth are needed for the basket challenge, a problem-solving game. Also, a laundry basket or bicycle basket or other see-through type of basket or box.

Dogs will display a variety of abilities in how they interact with toys, obstacles and problem-solving. For very fearful dogs, dogs afraid of objects, or those who guardian says "my dog doesn't play" make activity quite easy in the beginning and see how the dog progresses through the CED (See Chapter 10 Using Emotion in Play, Games and Problem-solving).

Alone time

Alone time during a CED is to allow a dog to deeply sleep. It is also to start to address attention seeking, separation anxiety and problem behavior. Provisions will have to be made for a dog if alone time is stressful to them. Setting the stage with a safe place where relaxation can be undisturbed is a key element. Where this place is could be a cozy crate, a bedroom with a baby gate, an xpen in main living area, or dog may be fine on a couch or on their own bed or mat. This area should be quiet during the CED, with minimal to no distractions.

Music is advised and is a tension releaser and relaxer for mind and body. It can be classical, or audio biotechnology for dogs, such as Through a Dog's Ear (see Resource section of this book under websites section) or music for dogs on YouTube.

Grooming tools

Grooming is a great way to increase a bond and relationship, but is also a much-needed husbandry exercise. It shows a lot about the guardian dog trust relationship. What is needed is a brush, a nail clipper, dreml or nail file, a toothbrush or finger brush and a calming shampoo.

Trainer may add or delete items depending on what is being seen with individual dog. There are no right or wrong answers in the CED. The main goal is to release stress, harmful body-wide toxins and getting a deep, refreshing REM sleep. Assessing patterns is secondary goal to observe how dog processes information, how they think, how they process sensory information, and can they problem-solve.

Chapter 5

The Right Combination

From sensory application to engaging the mind and brain in problem-solving activities, the Canine Emotional Detox (CED) provides the right combination of progressive elements to achieve stress release in challenging dogs in the form of a systematic process. -Diane Garrod

Trainers strive to be more effective in analyzing behavior, in getting faster results and helping dog guardians be compliant with ultimate goals of longer lasting results. All are good reasons to apply a systematic stress release process. Systematic means there is a step-by-step format. This will be more effective working with the client, so getting their buy-in to the process is important.

A partnership of dog, client, and trainer

Building a better relationship and bond between guardian and their dog, while creating a stress-free environment for a companion, foster or shelter dog, or solving high-level challenges, such as aggression, hyperactivity, high-level reactivity, sound sensitivities, OCD (obsessive compulsive disorders), separation anxiety and more, is a long-term CED goal. Knowing when to bring in a veterinarian, veterinarian behaviorist or other professional as a part of the team, making trainer's job easier and saving a canine life is ultimate and short-term CED goal.

The CED is that missing link to enhancing results of a successful behavior modification program to identifying skill deficits and seeking long term results for challenging dogs and their guardians. It encourages positive relations and teaches the guardian, while focusing on the dog as a unique individual. It releases stress toxins, tests problem-solving skills, and looks at other issues like focus, equilibrium, and the dog's environment.

Most of us jump right into behavior modification and skills training and sometimes results are less than convincing or lasting. Sometimes we have dogs so challenging we are afraid to set up a behavior change program or we assume euthanasia is the next step.

The systematic treatment process uses the right combination to neutralize bad stress chemicals from body and brain. A dog may not be in a state of learning yet due to acute or chronic stress in their lives. The CED provides a process, with the right combination of elements to de-stress the challenging canine and seamlessly lead trainer into an individualized behavior modification and skills applications process.

There are many studies, and books on stress and stress release, but there is nothing that explains an exact protocol to achieve deep sleep where stress release really starts to occur. The CED is that systematic stress release protocol. Everyone wants to know one thing, how to do the CED.

How does it work?

The simple answer is by using the right combination of elements. This book offers trainers working with highly challenging dogs, a how-to based on a circular, systematic cycle of stress release protocols that work repeatedly.

This systematic cycle covers six areas:

1. nutrition, health, and waste analysis

2. deep sleep and relaxation

3. importance of sensory proofing

4. learning through games and toys

5. physical movement instead of or in addition to exercise

6. problem-solving, how a dog thinks and copes

The CED looks at the dog from the inside outwardly, from diet to basic visual waste analysis, to release of stress chemicals within the body and brain and looks at how the dog learns and processes information. Looking at the CED as a three-day intensive stress release, a stress vacation, spa, pampering process plus a way to learn about, observe, analyze the individual dog puts the trainer and guardian on the right track. The end result is a high-end behavior modification plan in a final analysis format easy for guardian, trainer, and other professionals to decipher and implement.

Often, I hear of two-week plans that have sporadic pieces to the puzzle operating, such as some brain games, some relaxation, some exercise, but no system is in place. Then there are other trainers who do days and days of just relaxation or on the flip side a high level of exercise. The CED puts these into a formula, the right combination of elements to not only neutralize bad stress chemicals within an average 72-hour period, but to ultimately provide a dog's ideal day, postCED.

The right combination involves a circular cycle in an intensity to make real changes. Here is the visual of this protocol:

THE PATH OF THE CED
The Right Combination

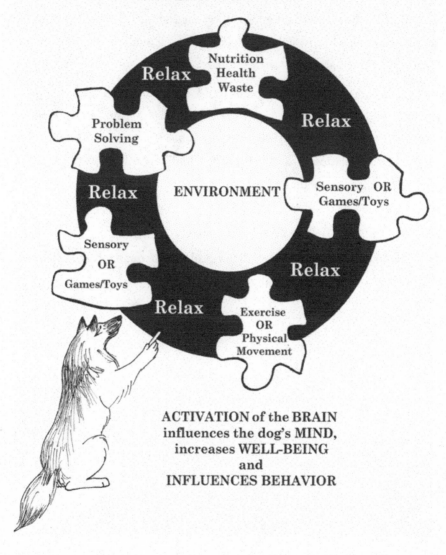

Relax — **Nutrition Health Waste**

Relax

Problem Solving

Relax — **ENVIRONMENT** — **Sensory OR Games/Toys**

Sensory OR Games/Toys

Relax

Relax — **Exercise OR Physical Movement**

**ACTIVATION of the BRAIN
influences the dog's MIND,
increases WELL-BEING
and
INFLUENCES BEHAVIOR**

Illustrator Carol Byrnes, Author of "What is my dog saying"; "What is my dog saying at the dog park" and "What is my cat saying" interactive PowerPoint CDs, available at www.dogwise.com. Carol is owner of Diamonds in the Ruff, Spokane, Washington State.

Simplistically, CED day is three cycles, day two, two cycles, and day one, one cycle. The white pieces can be added to, or stacked, if needed.

The CED is based on the concept that challenging dog's needs are not being satiated and causing them varying levels of continued stress. There is always a reason for why a behavior is being exhibited. The CED looks at the dog from the inside outwardly without being invasive or demanding.

During a CED the actual cycle may be repeated two or three times per day and five to seven times over a full 72-hour period. It is the intensity and order of this cycle that are key to achieving deep sleep. The, variables can change based on behavior witnessed. For example, a very hyperactive dog will have more activity, problem-solving steps to mentally tire.

It will take three days, at least, to neutralize stress chemicals depending on how distressed the dog. If they exhibit chronic stress during the process, day two is usually the time you might see an extinction burst or increase in bad behavior, then a longer process will be needed. What the dog was doing is no longer working, they are starting to feel differently, so they become either more persistent or try some other behavior. Some dogs will fight the process of relaxation, as feeling stressed has simply come to feel normal to them, habituated and deep sleep requires them to let their guard down. It is a normal part of the process.

Physical exercise is, of course, needed in a dog's daily life to meet the needs of and satiate a dog. However, if the physical exercise is stressful for the dog, it is counterproductive to improvement. The physical exercise element must be a stress reliever, not a stress enhancer for it to be included as a part of the CED process as part of the physical stimulation puzzle piece in the cycle. Physical exercise is a great way to release glucocorticoids (See Chapter 1, Let's talk about glucocorticoids section), but not if it is a stressful for the dog.

The CED clearly identifies problem areas but doesn't assume anything about the dog, the pet guardians or the environment.

The CED is a form of systematic desensitization

In humans, a systematic desensitization process consists of three components:

- deep relaxation training
- hierarchy of intensity of exposure to stimuli
- counterconditioning

In its simplest explanation, a canine emotional detox procedure consists of:

- deep, intense relaxation leading to deep sleep
- intense, mentally tiring games and activities
- and physical stimulation (as in bodywork, tension release) and/or exercise IF it doesn't cause stress

The difference between the human and dog model is that dogs are not exposed to their stimuli in the CED until postCED. There can be but there is usually no counter-conditioning element yet, unless a dog is over-barking, there is multi-dog household fighting tension or there is sensitivity to noises. The final analysis makes specific recommendations as to what to use when the behavior modification process is restarted or begun based on patterns seen during the CED. The CED is the perfect process to precede a behavior modification program and learn more about the dog, their environment and their situation before stimuli and counter conditioning is added.

Dogs, as individuals, first achieve deep sleep to ensure physiological changes within the body building good stress chemicals (eustress) for increased learning function. Preparing the dog's body from the inside out, fostering deep relaxation, and drawing the canine into a solid learning state means rehabilitation can occur faster and be longer lasting.

A case of hyperactivity with Weimaraner, Blue

Before

After

"Blue is more relaxed. I have learned that I need to keep her away from her "triggers" (i.e., the front windows) I also need to do more mentally (tiring) games with her." - Blue's guardian

The benefit of the CED is that not only does the trainer learn about the dog, but also about the pet guardian (personality, quirks, likes, dislikes, how they handle stress, how they learn, how they interact with their dog and what their relationship is with their dog). It also helps trainer learn about the environment from which the whole cycle revolves.

The three-day ideal goal is zero reactivity/aggression. A stress vacation to achieve deep sleep is main goal.

Day One

The first day out of three strives for complete relaxation where the dog works through a systematic process of rest, relax, calm. Looking for deep sighs is important during these relaxation periods and indicate the dog is releasing tension. Make it clear to the client to take digitals and video of relaxationperiods, and to record sighs. This stage is the chemical dump caused by elevated stress levels.

Day Two

The second and third days are customized as to what is being seen in day one. The goal is to take calm into non-REM, REM, non-REM, where sleep is so deep if guardian moves around, the dog remains sleeping. The reality of day two is it can get worse before it gets better, because the dog starts to feel differently, what worked before, no longer works, and routine has changed. It does not last long. If a dog is having trouble sleeping, then mentally tiring activities are increased.

CED findings have shown when the body neutralizes elevated stress neurotransmitters the similarity is like withdrawal symptoms from an addiction. Some dogs may experience none of the below symptoms indicating they are either simply distressed or on low end of acute stress. High stress withdrawal symptoms on day two might be headache, vomiting, shaking it off repeatedly (adrenalin rushes); irritability; anxiety; agitation; insomnia (resisting sleep/fighting it); stomach aches; increases in respiration and in rare cases depression. It depends on several factors, to include whether the dog is acutely stressed, chronically stressed and:

- if there are underlying medical conditions length of time dog has been stressed

- Mild symptoms would include headache, insomnia, anxiety, shaking it off, gastrointestinal disturbances and an increase in respiration.

- Moderate symptoms would include some of mild symptoms in addition to increased heart rate, confusion (or inability to learn, possibly brief shut down), diarrhea, and panting.

- Severe symptoms would be increased arousal, impaired attention, inability to concentrate, and in very rare cases seizures.

- Stress release is important in a results-oriented and progressive behavior modification process. Sleep Disturbances occur, changes in mood, but no dog in over 700 cases has ever needed more then two, three day CEDs, only 10%, while 90% can recover with three designated days and thereafter, prevention, management and supervision. A dog not anxious about inner noise can concentrate and participate fully in a designated learning plan.

Day Three

The third day is a wind down day and has a specific relax, activity format. Deep REM should be accomplished in day three, or the dog is in a chronic stress pattern where they are having a hard time coming out of it. Stress has levelled out over threshold and extended days are ideal, or another three day CED, one month later.

Chapter 6

The Dog Within

"Dogs do speak, but only to those who know how to listen."
– Orhan Pamuk, My Name is Red

What you do not see may be as important as what you do see. Jumping to conclusions from what is seen by behavior outwardly is common, and often is the first connection to working with a dog who has behavioral challenges. Modifications are based on techniques applied through those assumptions. How can we make a bigger difference in the dog's behavior change? By listening to the inner dog.

Listening to the inner dog

Here are some examples:

Nyx, Pitbull female, was outwardly hyperactive and in a constant state of extreme stress and high energy. What could not be seen was how Nyx felt having incontinence, leakage. As she relaxed muscles, leakage worsened in day two as body and muscles started to relax, which indicated she was always holding it in, creating tense muscles, and being on the go meant less leakage. Also meant more professional evaluation was needed. In consulting a veterinarian behaviorist the reply was, "

I would want this dog to have a thorough exam (hermaphrodites are more common than you think) and even if they didn't do any surgery, it would not cost too much to sedate her and get a good look at the situation. Also, PPA (Proin) can be life-saving in these cases."

During Dachshund Rusty's CED, something on Rusty's "right side" of body just between last rib and rear leg thighs looked off. It looked wider on that side in movement videos and there were two distinct bumps there. In a movement exercise, it was also noted that his left leg was moving a bit differently than the rest of his legs. His pet guardian, Lynda McCormick (see her illustration of Chancellor at end of this book) said there were some right sided leg concerns so he just may be compensating for this by putting more pressure on his left leg. Worth checking it out. Rusty passed away in early 2017 from cancer.

Subie, an Irish Wolfhound was resource guarding toward guardians and other dogs in household. Internally events were happening that would change everything and make resource guarding irrelevant. He eventually had his spleen removed and had to have liters of blood as his red blood cells were being eaten. He was diagnosed with an unusual cancer of the liver and mesentery on top of the autoimmune problems he had developed. He left this earth 9/18/2014.

Bindi, a Jack Russell Terrier, was excitable, whiny, bouncy, humping arms, was dog reactive, and could not settle. She would pick food out of her bowl and take it to another location. She had known allergies. Today, Bindi enjoys proper nutrition, calming exercises, body alignment, acupuncture and chiropractic visits all a result of findings from her CED. She is healthier physically, as well as emotionally.

Her guardian said: "Her emotional detox was intense but I could not have been happier with the results, it was so worth it and has done so much for our family and for Bindi, I would (and will) continue to do it for her and for our other dogs on a regular basis." (See more on Bindi, page 60)

Buster, rescued Shih Tzu, was a biter, a rescue, and was one paw away from being put to sleep. After his CED it was recommended he have a chiropractic visit and to keep pressure away from his neck, meaning during touch, no collar grabbing and no prolonged petting in the neck area. Buster had been on a shock collar prior to coming to his new home, and his neck was more sensitive as a result. With improved nutrition, a chiropractic adjustment and positive reinforcement training, Buster is a different dog today biting is a behavior of the past. He is a real joy to his family.

In all the cases above, what we cannot see also matters.

The importance of the dog within

Below are all the elements the trainer will and should analyze during the CED. Waste and pH urine is checked and compared in days one and three. This will all be a part of the biologics review in the final analysis of the CED and determine whether other professionals need to be brought in.

How to check biologics

Despite the wealth of scientific information about the dog — about how they see, smell, hear, look, learn — there are places science doesn't travel. On matters of personality, personal experience, emotions, and simply what they think about, science is quiet. Still, the accumulation of data about dogs provide a good foothold from which to extrapolate and reach toward answers to those questions. Alexandra Horowitz, Author of Inside of a Dog, What Dogs See, Smell and Know

Discovering the dog within during a CED includes those functions easy to measure and cost-effective. Those areas include: a visual analysis of the dog's waste, vomit (if present), taking a respiration level and looking at current nutrition.

Waste and pH urine strips

Checking a dog's waste is a big and easy-to-assess part of the CED process. It can indicate when a veterinarian check is needed through color, consistency, contents, and coating. A guardian can take prevention measures with a simple waste check, a pH urine strip sample that could lead to a veterinarian visit and a fecal sample and/or blood work as a baseline for future blood work. It is a critical factor to assure the dog is in good health.

Canine Detoxification Diet

In addition, the digestion process is also vitally important and looking at how food passes through the body can alert the dog pet guardian to issues such as stomach distress, parasites, diseases, and pain. The detox annotation of the canine emotional detox denotes gut health, digestion, eating patterns, all which can affect how a dog progresses and processes information.

The importance of digestion in dogs

In the how to portion of the CED, the first relaxation period in the Canine Emotional Detox is a 20-minute rest period AFTER eating breakfast in the first day. Thereafter, 20 minutes AFTER exercising and/or 20 minutes after eating to relax and digest their food properly. Most guardians do not allow for this process and may, in fact, exacerbate health problems without knowing it. Immediately after eating a dog may be let out to potty and to bark at passers-by, or to play with housedogs. This can result in disrupting the digestive process and lead to stomach aches, gas, burping etc. The CED allows the dog to relax and to comfortably start the digestion process first. Stress goes right to the stomach.

In all, the entire digestion process, from the time a dog bites into his food to the time waste is produced, can take anywhere from around 10 hours to a couple of days to complete the digestion process. This fits perfectly into a three-day stress release protocol. A waste picture will be taken in day one, recording what was put into system up to two days prior. Another is taken in day three to compare and will reflect the detoxification diet waste.

A dog's stomach will work on breaking down food for approximately eight hours before passing it into the small intestine. The broken down food will remain in the intestine for about two days, depending on how difficult it is to break it down. Whatever remains when small intestine is finished is passed to the large intestine and processed in a few hours, according to Vet Med, Washington State University (www.vetmed.wsu.edu).

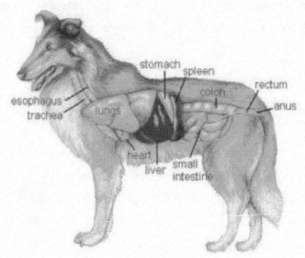

www.vetmed.wsu.edu

The CED detoxification diet follows a traditional illness diet protocol that might be recommended by a veterinarian. It is best to check with a veterinarian to assess for dogs who are on specialized veterinarian- recommended diets or for dogs on medication, injections, or have medical issues before proceeding (see chapter 5 for details).

The goal is that the dog is satiated and what that looks like for each individual. Satiation reduces blood flow and oxygen to the brain as the body diverts resources to digestion (therefore, the importance of a 20M digestion relaxation period after eating). The CED addresses the building of serotonin and melatonin levels through encouraging deep sleep where these are restored, especially in non-REM sleep stage.

Choosing the meats for the CED is based on the need for protein by the dog and that people don't have to break the bank to buy chicken, or turkey top two on the list. Some dogs with allergies may need to stick to fish-based foods or continue their current diets. Fish that can be used is halibut, mackerel, sardines, salmon, cod. Cod is especially good for dogs with neurological issues/seizures as it naturally contains taurine. Taurine is an amino acid that supports neurological development and helps regulate the level of water and minerals in the blood. Taurine is also thought to have antioxidant properties and is found naturally in meat and fish.

Carbohydrates in foods such as rice, quinoa lead to a relatively wider fluctuation in circulating insulin levels. This more likely leads to becoming tired, and feeling good from the inside out, similar to what humans feel after a large, celebratory dinner.

Fiber foods should be organic. The food detox cleans out body waste deposits, so dog isn't running with a dirty engine or functioning with the brakes on. What occurs during a digestive detoxification is the digestive tract is cleansed of accumulated waste and fermenting bacteria. Excess mucous and congestion is cleared from body, and mental clarity is enhanced, which is less likely and even impossible under chemical over-load. Gut health is important in humans and canines for optimal function. Recent advances in molecular methods have revealed that the canine and feline gastrointestinal tract harbors a complex microbial ecosystem, com-prising several hundred different bacterial genera.

Mood changes affecting behavior can be due to stomach distress, con-stipation, diarrhea and full anal sacs. Itchiness can be one indication of digestive issues.

In day two of the CED, an energy-building carbohydrate is included, such as an orange or yellow vegetable and in day three a canine acceptable green vegetable, such as broccoli, brussels sprouts, dark greens, or green beans replaces the orange or yellow vegetable. Each also represents a sen-sory exercise of taste, sweet and sour.

A huge part of the CED is to bring other professionals into the process, as needed on a per dog basis, such as a canine nutrition expert, veteri-narians, veterinarian behaviorist, veterinarian chiropractor, veterinarian ophthalmologist, holistic veterinarian, and other professionals as pat-terns begin to emerge from the CED. This is a critical piece to the puzzle and allows a dog's pet guardian, trainer, behavior consultant to use, sug-gest and recommend medical professionals based on patterns emerging where further analysis would be beneficial and required. The CED is only a launching point, not a diagnosis. Further testing may be required by the skilled eyes of medical and/or other relevant canine professional. Leave the medical analysis to the medical professionals.

Looking for and deciphering patterns to better understand the dog as an individual is an emphasis in the CED and to creating a final analysis. Over an intense three-day stress release period analysis focuses on several pieces to discover the dog within, such as, how does the dog rest and relax, how long does it take to achieve deep REM (restless eye movement) sleep, how long does it take for the dog to settle, how do they solve problems, how do they think things through, what emotions are coming through during the CED. To assess this, mentally tiring activities are completed using a dog's senses, smell, auditory, visual, touch and perception to help achieve deep relaxation that results in REM sleep.

Physical activity during CED

The physically tiring aspect of the process uses alternatives to physical exercise. These would be activities such as obstacle coursework, mini-homemade-agility where a look at the dog's movement is analyzed while the dog is having fun. This might also include a simple walk up and back several times in front of the camera. All these exercises are videotaped and digitally photographed.

Relaxation periods to achieve deep sleep

Relaxation happens in stages. One point that needs clarifying about deep relaxation is that it is a process. It cannot be rushed, it must occur naturally. Some dogs will fight fully relaxing, especially if they are in chronic stress, never have regular relaxation periods without distraction, have a lot of external input and are unable to calm down. It will feel odd to completely achieve deep relaxation, but is all the more reason it is needed.

Bindi – Parsons Russell Terrier – Case – Allergies

Discovering the dog within and how and why that was important in Bindi's case.

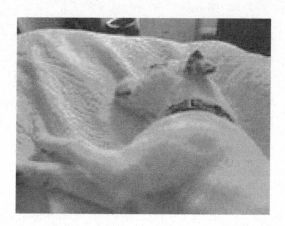

Bindi's initial behaviors were described as excitable, whiny, bouncy. She was arm humping, dog reactive, Had issues in a multi-dog household, as well as allergies. Bindi just could not settle.

After the CED, Bindi was calmer and more tolerant of the other dogs in the household. Her pet guardian says:

"Bindi is a different dog since her emotional detox than she was in the prior 5 years of her life, even now, months later. She is more content, she sleeps through the night and sleeps in almost every morning. She is so much more tolerant of the other dogs and even initiates play with them almost daily, but does not get overly aroused or out of control, and very rarely snarks at them. She enjoys the outdoors more now as well as she worries less, she is no longer hyper-vigilant and reactive to every little sound she hears, she gets excited to be out, but still checks in with us and is easily called away from things. She is much more pleasant to be around for all of us. She loves to play games that she learned during her detox, but has even better self-control now. Bindi really enjoys her new diet and her acupuncture and chiropractic visits, which are all a result of findings from her CED and she is healthier physically as well as emotionally. Her CED was intense, but I could not have been happier with

the results, it was so worth it and has done so much for our family and for Bindi, I would (and will) continue to do it for her and for our other dogs on a regular basis." **Alyson Brown, CPDT Sept. 28, 2012**

Bindi postCED getting along with a puppy

Bindi through the years

"Bindi had dog issues, this last photo wouldn't have been possible prior to her CED. The puppy in the last photo is a 5-month-old Beagle, female. Bindi had problems with all sorts of dogs, but females were a major issue for her. She turned seven in October 2013, and prior to her CED we could not have had another female dog in our household. Since then we've been able to have friends visit with their dogs, and had a female foster dog that ended up staying permanently. She will be three this year and Bindi's favorite playmate. There is still plenty of management that goes on in our household, but considering where we started, I wouldn't have put it past her to kill another dog under the right circumstances, and certainly a rodent, and that the management needed now is minimal we couldn't be happier with where she is now." **Alyson Brown, CPDT, pet guardian, February 7, 2014 update**

Discovering why a dog is distressed leads to eventually creating a results-oriented behavior modification process. Is the dog fearful and of what? Are they hyper-sensitive to sudden environmental changes? Do they run away from new objects? Do they have a relationship with the pet guardian? How does the pet guardian interact with the dog? What body language is being seen? How does the dog respond to routine changes? Does the dog have any cold or hot spots, painful areas, stomach aches, gas, burping and how do they move? All is important to solving the puzzle of stress release and behavior change. What emotional struggles are observed?

Chapter 7

Emotional Land Mines

The science behind dogs and emotion

Scientists have a responsibility to convey as much as they know about the reality of canine emotions, guiding pet guardians to a proper perception of what their dogs can and cannot feel.

- John Bradshaw, Dog Sense

Canine emotions have been studied for ages. Pavlov discovered a dog feels viscerally, physically connected to what they are attracted to. It makes sense to equate that learning more about what the dog is feeling internally will give insight into how to create new associations externally as a part of a results-oriented behavior modification program.

Behavioral challenges occur for a reason. The CED attempts to neutralize stress chemicals while gathering insight into the dog from the inside outwardly. Since that is the case, it is also a process of analysis, observation and discovering patterns.

Emotions and feelings, do dogs have them?

Positive emotions arising in connection with the perfection of a skill, irrespective of its pragmatic significance at a given moment, serve as the reinforcement." - Simonov, Pavel Vasil'evich

Simonov, Pavlov's assistant discovered emotion to be object-oriented evidenced by the fact that the strongest emotional responses are elicited by external objects (prey/play/mate/offspring/toy). External stimuli trigger visceral, autonomic responses over which an animal has no control and satisfying the internal void (physical/sexual/social appetite) requires an external object.

What are canine emotions and feelings? Do dogs have emotions? Why is this important to the CED?

Charles Darwin saw emotional expression as an outward communication of an inner state, and the form of that expression often carries beyond its original adaptive use.

Since Pavlov and Darwin, the scientific study of emotions in dogs has gone from the 20th Century and the dawn of the hard behavioral scientist movement, spearheaded by behavioral psychologists like Watson, who considered any kind of mind/mental/cognitive states as irrelevant, unscientific clutter. Instead they concentrated on stimulus-response behaviors that could be measured. Consensus among neuroscientists working with human and/or non-human subjects is that only humans are conscious. (Panksepp, 2005a) Throughout the 19th Century many scientists accepted the concept of the mind, emotions, and feelings as psychological phenomena.

Luckily, the pendulum swings and over the last 25 years and into the 21st Century neuroscientists have contributed a vast amount of information on emotional learning and on the neurophysiology of fear in particular.

Five basic emotions are what we, as humans, think of in relation to dogs. They are fear, joy, pain, grief and anger. However, Jaack Panksepp has a different scale and describes seven emotions. They are seeking, rage, fear, lust, care, panic, and play.

A dog's personality

Not only is each dog an emotional being, but each dog has its own sensitive personality. A personality describes the individual as unique. Emotions determine how a dog behaves in certain situations. Fight, flight, freeze and fidget/fool around are emotional responses that come forward through high level stress.

The CED focuses on relieving the dog of negative sensations and replacing them with positive sensations through relaxation, mentally tiring activities, sensory exercises, and physical stimulation. If dogs learn by association and consequence, it is not a stretch to understand why the CED is effective.

Emotions can take a toll on how a dog responds daily from tense, agitated, over-sensitive, anxious and hyperactive to becoming a more confident, calm, relaxed and responsive member of the family. Emotion describes the dog's personality, which can be vital in determining a behavior modification process that will be effective for the individual. The end result of the CED is a Final Analysis, an individualized behavior modification document.

If inner emotions can be transformed and associations changed, then a dog's behavior will change, stress will be released and the bad emotions will be replaced with the good emotions.

Milo's Story

Milo enjoying a warm towel

Milo with a warm towel as a sensory piece prior to relaxation. However, as is seen if the sensory application is successful, relaxation will be easier and may occur immediately. Making note of where the warmth is applied is also key, as this may indicate an area of pain, or digestive distress or a former injury.

In the case of Milo, a dog reactive black Labrador Retriever mix, chronic stress made it clear he would need two three-day CEDs before he was ready to begin any type of behavior modification related to his dog and environmental reactivity. This determination was made based on the fact that he could not achieve deep sleep during the first 72 hours. Ten percent of dogs are like Milo, chronically stressed.

During the first CED we learned he did not have good foundational skills. There was a lot of preliminary work to bring Milo into a state-of-mind to learn. One month after CED 1, Milo's pet guardian Liz, Arizona reported,

"Milo is doing so very much better and I wanted to share that with you. I have changed our routine significantly because of our work with you & (Milo's trainer). I've got him back on a diet (he needs to lose 10 lbs.! vet appointment with a Thyroid test is scheduled). We're focusing on relaxation work (wraps, TTouch, the labyrinth/obstacle course and rest periods). He is sleeping longer and better/deeper. I've had a couple of friends drop by and they have commented on how relaxed he seems to them. While he is still barking at the doorbell (and I am working with him on the 3-bark rule), generally his barking is significantly reduced. Another thing that is markedly less is his eating of poop when we go on our walk each day. Yeah!!

We're also playing games together just for fun – treat bowling, catch, find it, and hide & seek. This is a joy for both of us! And I've been leaving him Kongs and/or one of his treat puzzles when I go to work. I'm still working on improving my handling skills (one of my friends commented – helpfully- on my need to enunciate more clearly), and I'm using the clicker more. I could go on and on (happily) and I want you to know that I am finding your report and analysis incredibly helpful – thank you again." Liz

In Milo's case, a veterinarian was needed as part of his behavior change team. Liz worked with her Trainer, Cricket Mara, in Arizona on Milo's behavior modification change program.

The CED is a great way to pick out patterns and build a knowledge base of the dog as an individual, as well as the dog pet guardian and/or family, the environment. The CED:builds knowledge of the canine, their environment, their family provides deeper insights so behavior can change, effectively provides long-lasting results and creates a final analysis as the basis for a behavior modification and skills deficits process. It can help identify health issues making it clear if other professionals need to be brought into help with the process.

The Dog's Brain – the information and emotion center

"Behavioral systems are reluctant to change without compelling need. Behavioral adjustment depends on learning, but learning is possible only to the extent that an animal is biologically equipped and prepared to learn. The organization of behavior is genetically programmed to be flexible and variable but only to a certain extent and according to more or less fixed laws and parameters of change defined by the brain and senses. In essence, the brain and senses biologically define the limits of what an animal can learn and how it can learn it, while experience dictates the moment-to-moment direction of those changes. Survival depends on an animal's ability to learn from its experiences, to adjust its behavior in accordance with what it has learned, and to form a set of reliable predictions and strategies of control that enable it to encounter similar circumstances most effectively in the future." Lindsay, Neurobiology of Behavior and Learning Vol. 1, 2000

The dog's brain is like the human brain, except the cortex is smaller, but the brain is just as complex. Dogs can make decisions and problem-solve. Stress puts a dog into survival mode where making good decisions and problem-solving and thinking can be impaired. A dog's behavior may start to change because actual cell make-up has changed.

Wally's Story

Here is the story of Wally, who along with socialization deficits, was stressed and extremely fearful. Avoidance and hiding was a part of his daily routine. Wally, a Lab/Rhodesian Ridgeback/Pitbull mix is an example of how small steps lead to big changes in the brain.

Wally before – the journey of a fearful/feral dog and those who love him

Wally spent his days as a pup under a deck with his mother and siblings. When the dogs were found and relocated to a county shelter, Wally was the only survivor. At three-months-old, he found himself in a new environment. He curled up in a corner, fearful of everyone and everything, until a shelter volunteer took an interest in him, and eventually became his pet guardian.

Wally's behavior prior to a CED process was hiding in the back bedroom, barking at the male in the household, having no relationship with male in household, ready to flee at any moment should he come out of the room. Wally was a dog with extreme fear and he was intensely bonded to the female pet guardian who adopted him.

Wally's CED was four and a half days and completed on 9/06/2012. It was completed in two parts, a one and a half day (not a typical process, CED had to be aborted first round) but full three days were rescheduled and completed.

Wally AFTER

The changes afterwards were a multitude, and are relayed numerically and in the pet guardian's words.

1. Strengthened (an even stronger) a bond between them.

2. Provided a layer of trust that was not there before the CED.

3. The fact that Wally performed mentally stimulating exercises – that he had never done before – were like an ah ha moment.

4. Realized Wally responds well to laughter and now has a true happiness about him.

5. Now he loves physical touch and seeks it out.

6. His confidence is building and he is less reliant on house brother, Murray, a border collie. His pet guardian admits in the early stages Murray's interactions with them and Wally were priceless and necessary in getting Wally to trust and learn. He has since been able to function without Murray's presence. The CED started him on that journey and as time progressed, a different dog emerges.

7. People are noticing – Wally goes up to people now at the dog parks; and will take treats.

8. Interactions are better with male spouse today, but Wally is cautious about letting him (or other men) touch or pet him. It is evident from Wally's case and hundreds of others, it is not only about the dog, but about the human end of the equation. How all family members are interacting with the dog is equally as important to success in behavior change.

9. Wally is not barking anymore at male pet guardian when he comes home; stands in doorways; or comes down a hallway – HUGE PROGRESS.

This was very problematic earlier and, in fact, the reason a behavior consultant was called in the first place. Wally will now jump on bed with both pet guardians and will allow a pet from the male pet guardian.

*Confident Transformations Class postCED: Meeting a male stranger;
With pet guardians weaving through cones; Working in discovery exercise*

Wally progressed enough by April 10, 2013 to take and finish a seven and a six-week Confident Transformations Class respectively for fearful dogs at Canine Transformations Learning Center.

He is now seeking out the company of the male spouse and criteria has been raised to the point that now a treat is earned for a pet under the chin or to side of cheek.

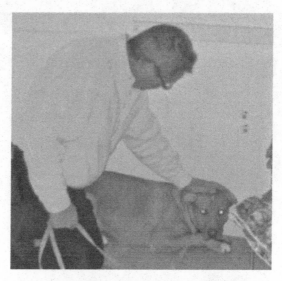

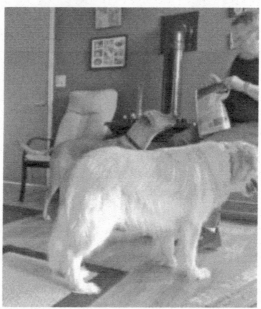

Wally with male guardian before and after postCED Confident Transformations Class. In first Confident Transformations class, still worried, progressing to second photo showing graduation in sixth week.

What does the brain have to do with it?

How the dog processes information, thinks, feels, what chemicals rush through has everything to do with the brain and internal versus external functioning of the canine. Often, we look only outwardly and then apply a behavior and skills plan based on what we see. What we can't see is often as important, if not more important than what is visually portrayed and vital to success. What we visually see is the behavior that surfaces, important, but not always the whole story.

"Of several responses made to the same situation, those that are accompanied or closely followed by satisfaction to the animal will, with other things being equal, be more firmly connected to a situation so that when it recurs they will be more likely to recur." Edward Thorndike

"If you do something and it feels good, you'll do more of it." Jaak Panksepp (in translation of Edward Thorndike's quote)

Subtle shifts in brain chemistry will alter behavior, alter mood, alter concentration, and alter memory. As an example, chronic stress, as in chronic exposure to one of the stress chemicals does different things in different regions of the brain. In the hippocampus, crucial for learning and memory, chronic stress results in decreased synaptic plasticity. Synaptic plasticity means the neurons are less dense and connected.

In the amygdala, the part of the mammalian brain responsible for processing emotions, handling fearful experiences and stimuli, an increase in synaptic plasticity and function is seen during chronic stress.

Chronic stress shrinks the part of the brain needed to learn and remember and on the flip side expands the part of the brain that helps process fearful stimuli. Stress itself is not creating new neuronal pathways, but it IS influencing the function of what is already there.

Stress during canine development, however, does influence how the brain develops. Stress during early life (pre- or post-natal) can, and does, play a big part in how the actual stress-axis (and stress response) develops.

Chronic stress during this time point will often serve to 'sensitize' the amygdala region of the brain. This part of the brain is always working, scouring the environment to assess potential threats etc. Under chronic stress conditions, this region becomes 'sensitized'. In people with over-active amygdala you see enhanced vigilance and fear responses. A dog with an overactive or sensitized amygdala will have a greater likelihood of perceiving a non-threatening or neutral stimulus as threatening. (Francis, Darlene, Neurobiologist)

Understanding changes within the dog are occurring, brain and body, allows an understanding of why stress release is important. Taking a look at the dog within, can be an important key to solving behavioral issues.

This chart lists the top seven challenging dog behaviors the CED has worked with; the top three medications dogs were already on before a CED was conducted; the top seven known health issues the dogs had prior to a CED and issues discovered during the CED that indicated veterinarian attention was needed. Note: Chart is a list only, not a relational chart, columns do not relate to each other.

Behavior	Known Meds	Known Health	Discovered Health or Future
Dog dog	Prozac	Allergies	Hypothyroid
Dog human	Fluoxetine	Ear Infections	Chiropractic
Sound/Envir	Heartworm meds	Anxiety	Parasites
Bite history		Copraphagia	Blood workup
Multi-dog household fighting		Hip Dysplasia	Stomach issues
Extreme Fear		Diahrrea	Impacted Anal Sacs
Resource Guarding		Arthritis	Urinalysis

Health issues in last column were a result of postCED veterinarian examination based on discoveries in the final analysis. All these issues can be a reason a dog is irritable, dysfunctional, highly stressed and having challenges in the first place. The very pieces that can relieve stress when taken care of and change behavior to those areas that are not visible outwardly. Behavior challenges may require a team.

Chapter 8

How to use emotion in play, games and problem-solving

Here is a guideline on how the CED uses Panksepp's seven emotional systems in play, games, and problem-solving, 2005a, 2005b, as a guide. In the CED pathway, the suggested games by emotion below can be slotted into the problem-solving piece of the pathway depending on what is being seen in the dog's behavior profile. The ideas listed in this chapter can also be used daily to normalize stress levels.

Explanations of each emotion is followed by recommended problem-solving activities. These activities can be used, inserted into the white sections of the CED cycle found in Chapter five, The Right Combination.

Seeking System

What is the seeking system? The seeking system deals with the brain's anatomy.

"Although the details of human hopes are surely beyond the imagination of other creatures, the evidence now clearly indicates that certain intrinsic aspirations of all mammalian minds, those of mice as well as men, are driven by the same ancient neurochemistries." Jack Panksepp

In description, the seeking system is actually the mesolimbic and mesocortical dopamine pathways, which Panksepp explains "tend to energize and coordinate the functions of many higher brain areas that mediate planning and foresight (such as the amygdala, nucleus accumbens, and frontal cortex)." Some stressed dogs have a too pronounced urge to use their seeking system to the exclusion of everything else in their environment.

Dopamine is the primary neurotransmitter operative in the seeking system. In humans, too much dopamine is cause for schizophrenia, while low levels result in depression and anxiety. In animals, Panksepp states, when animals are in an appetitive state, anticipating a reward such as food or sex with a receptive mate, dopamine levels increase. But once an appetitive state turns into a consummatory state, dopamine levels immediately begin to decrease. Increasing levels of dopamine are not associated with consummatory, pleasurable activity. Pleasure is associated with decreasing dopamine levels.

"Temporal and frontal cortices contain an abundance of neurons that fire only in response to stimuli that have acquired meaning by being predictably associated with rewards." Panksepp suggests that the SEEKING system "responds not simply to positive incentives but also to many other emotional challenges where animals must seek solutions."

Puzzles, problem-solving games can satisfy the seeking system.

The games and problem-solving activities below can be used in the CED systematic cycle. Review the list and put in at the appropriate section. The individual dog's emotional state can determine which game or problem-solving activity will satisfy them and mentally tire.

Games/problem-solving to satisfy the seeking system

Seeking activated

Use brain games geared toward, in the case of purebred dogs, what the breed was bred to do, such as herding, hunting etc.

- use a remote control toy or car to satisfy need to chase
- flirt poles or bungy tugs for chase and grab/shake or just grab/shake sequences
- take and give for a retrieving activity on and off switch games such as "Go Wild and Freeze" developed by Shelton, Washington trainer, September Morn
- foraging activities where dogs hunt for food or items. Use Easter eggs, egg cartons or other objects to hold food and hide them all over the house or yard, as seen in this video of my own dogs, and a friend, yard hunting https://www.youtube.com/watch?v=SMX9JfaQMfg
- tunneling
- ball and Frisbee activities
- obstacle course and/or fun agility set-ups
- problem-solving mentally stimulating activities – be creative, search dog game books like "How Dogs Think" by Immanuel Birmelin or "Brain Games" by Claire Arrowsmith

For the nature of the CED, activating the seeking system is a therapeutic process.

In animals the genesis of many behavior problems is the lack of opportunity. Some initially fear-related aggression problems in dogs turn in to 'addictive', dopamine-driven pleasure-seeking behaviors as their nucleus accumbens are flooded with dopamine.

If the seeking system is overactive or in obsessive compulsive output, then activities in this emotion would be minimized or not done at all during stress release protocol. It can cause an over-surge of dopamine, which is something to diminish during stress release not encourage and increase. If the dog needs to activate their seeking system or uses it for the feel good problem-solving of it and is not obsessive compulsive (OCD) about it, then you will want to use this emotion in the games and activities chosen. Stimulation of the seeking system prompts an animal into an appetitive search strategy.

Fear – Games and problem-solving to build confidence

Obstacle work for focus

The underlying fight/flight mechanism is the same in all mammals as mapped out by LeDoux, 1996. In comparison to a canine's experience with fear, a human's experience is similar. When a person looks at the world, he or she is confronted with an overwhelming amount of sensory information—sights, sounds, smells, and so on. After being processed in the brain's sensory areas, the information is relayed to the amygdala, which acts as a portal to the emotion-regulating limbic system.

Using input from the individual's stored knowledge, the amygdala determines how to respond emotionally, for example, with humans experiencing fear (at the sight of a burglar), or lust (on seeing a lover) or indifference (when facing something trivial). Messages cascade from the amygdala to the rest of the limbic system and eventually reach the autonomic nervous system, which prepares the body for action. If the person is confronting a burglar, heart rate will rise and body will sweat to dissipate the heat from muscular exertion. The autonomic arousal, in turn, feeds back into the brain, amplifying the emotional response. Over time, the amygdala creates a salience landscape, a map that details the emotional significance of everything in the individual's environment.

The hypothalamus and limbic system are responsible for sexual behaviors, hunger and thirst, thermoregulatory function, and also influence many aspects of emotional expression such as anger, rage, placidity, fear and social attraction.

The limbic system is comprised of the amygdala, hippocampus, mamillary bodies, hypothalamus, and other neurological structures. It operates by influencing the endocrine system and the autonomic nervous system.

Perceived fear stays deep in the mid-brain, i.e. a fear of thunderstorms or fireworks. A signal from a sudden noise arrives at the auditory thalamus that relays the data on to the sensory auditory cortex. Studies in neuroplasticity, the brain's adaptability, have proved that repeated experiences actually change the physical structure of the brain. Emergency info coming in goes immediately to amygdala as a matter of life and death.

The games that take the dog out of their comfort zone and allow them to experience new tasks, to think for themselves, and to experience new "feelings" or create alternate input can also increase confidence. Confidence building games should be done slowly and only as much as the dog can handle and in some cases, the objects in the games, desensitized before even attempting the game, depending on level of fear seen.

Confidence building activities are the primary choice, but foraging activity, activating the seeking system, is also good for fearful dogs. To determine what to use in CED, focus on confidence building games that define specific triggers, what dog feels safe working on, and let the fearful dog set the tone for what they can or cannot do by breaking problem-solving into small, easy-to-do steps.

Fearful Duncan and intelligence games. Duncan used to be very worried in the classroom, he could not even walk on the floors. Now, he has got games to satisfy his mind and take the focus off the scary environment. (RIP Duncan, October 2020)

Here are some examples of confidence building games, activities and problem-solving: obstacle coursework (see website links in Resource section) easy, homemade, basic agility, K9 Conditioning exercises (see website links in Resource section) relationship and bond building activities, interactive with human – cup games, putting a reward on a strip of cloth and covering it with a non-moveable cover (dog must pull out reward by studying and discovering the reward is on the cloth); color recognition; size recognition and more help build relationships that have eroded target/ touch exercises – simple touch and treat game, or treat toss on ground shaping exercises, esp. 101 things to do with a box any find it and nose work games purchased or homemade intelligence games worked behind a safety barrier.

Logan (extreme fear) easy steps. Breaking a task into something easy to do sets the dog up for success. Here instead of putting the reward UNDER the cup, it is easily accessible placed in the cup. In the CED it is very important to reduce complexity of an activity if dog is fearful.

For fearful dogs, building confidence means breaking down steps into easy to complete successes. Starting with the easiest puzzles or homemade games, like a muffin tin filled with balls and food under the balls or a braid filled with treats, a dog's confidence can improve and for fearful dogs that is key to building confidence and thriving not just surviving. Some dogs are not able to do puzzles at first or even foraging games. Breaking down the games into very tiny pieces to accomplish successfully builds the dog's confidence to try ever harder problem-solving.

Rage – Games and problem-solving to redirect thinking

Search as redirect games. Skye five time face biter.

Rage is like an immediate tantrum, an emotion elicited by direct brain stimulation. It can be dog to dog aggression, dog to human, leash aggression or a mental disorder. It is important, before moving on to develop a stress release protocol that defines specific triggers, to see what neutralizes it or if it is a health issue and to ask, what does the dog love to do and how can they be successful. This is an intense emotion and needs further exploration to determine viability of a CED. What is the dog angry or enraged about? What triggers it? Has a vet check eliminated a health issue?

Redirect games are great for these issues. One option is the '**go find it**' activity. Throwing food on the ground, left then right, one after the other and saying 'go find' each time encourages engagement and redirects mind to a pleasurable activity. Any games or activities that encourage 'go find it' can be used here and so any activities mentioned under the seeking system emotion are appropriate. The actual movement towards the food motivator is redirecting this dog's energy into something positive versus maintaining focus on the negatives in the environment causing them to react.

Search, such as in a kibble/meat hide is another redirect game. Dog is in a sit or down/stay. Let him/her see you hide one piece of kibble under a cup on the floor. Tell him/her to "take it, or search" and when he/she noses or knocks over the cup let him/her eat the reward. Once good at this practice or warm-up, then the kibble hide can be advanced. Hide food under two cups, then three, then expand and hide cups around the room, the house, the yard. Search will come to mean a fun game and can be used to redirect behavior.

Treat/Retreat, where the dog gets to decide to come forward to eat tossed reward or not. Human can toss treat and walk away and repeat. This is a simple game of toss the treat and either human can retreat, dog can choose to take treat or not, or dog can take treat and move away.

Many dogs do not know how to play or were discouraged from playing. The dog may have become afraid to play and so this takes the edge off. A regular, several minutes long play time with a start cue and an end cue can make playtime something to look forward to no matter where the dog is in that learning curve. At first, the dog might not play at all. But with time and variety, toy play becomes something to look forward to and enjoy. It is a great laboratory for real life learning.

Isaac foraging game. Human reactive, Isaac, solves a foraging game while a stranger is 10-feet away

Human reactive dogs can benefit in redirecting how a dog approaches a human, and games can be used to make humans less worrisome. A foraging game or intelligence game is set up between person and dog. Dog is on leash at first and has been pre-acclimated to games. Distance and duration are always key elements, incrementally increasing or decreasing. Dog approaches the game, as Isaac is doing in photo above, interacts with it while human is present at a predetermined distance that keeps the dog successful. This activity can be used later in a behavior modification process to help with pleasant approaches, no reactions and pairing something good (Counter Conditioning), the rewards under the cups for example, with something scary (approaching humans).

Evaluate how stressed the dog is, as this emotion may take a gradual adaptation to the activity to achieve successful exposure and willing participation. Keep distance at the forefront, gradually decreasing distance until success is achieved. Participation is still achieved if the dog at first can just look at the object, come over to see what it is and retreat. Always ask where the dog is in the process and create activity to meet that level of participation.

Lust – Games and problem-solving to reduce hyperactivity

Lust is self-explanatory. It is more than just between male and female. My own Kody Bear's default stress behavior was humping. Lust is defined as highly suggestive, erotic feelings awfully hard to ignore.

Object naming

Exercises to focus on are those that have cue development. Cues are important in redirecting the dog into other more acceptable activities than humping. We have all seen the dogs who sits and just stares and humps, or the dog that humps the toy or worse, another weaker dog who doesn't communicate to back off. So lust is more than just during estrous and can be directed toward either sex or an object or someone's leg. It is also a sign of an over-excitable dog, and/or boredom, but still falls under lust category as an emotion.

Object naming. This is an exercise to increase dog's vocabulary by teaching to retrieve a toy by name. Start with one favorite toy. Say name of this toy, and then ask dog to touch or to get this toy just named. Then take that toy away and work on a second favorite. Say name of this toy, and then ask dog to touch or to get this toy by name. Then add the two toys together and place about five feet apart in front of dog, who can be on a sit or down stay. Reward correct choices with food, or toy play. Once two toys are solid, take those away and teach names of two more objects separately, then together. Once those two are solid, bring out one of previous toys and ask for object by name with three in a row. If there is 80% success, then add fourth.

Rewarding good behaviors. Rewarding NOT humping and making good decisions. Keeping frustration and arousal levels low are key to working successfully with a dog showing these emotions.

Care – Games and problem-solving to change behavior

Care as in the whelping bitch triggered by levels of estrogen, progesterone, prolactin, and oxytocin, gives the mother the innate ability to care for her young (Panksepp, 2006). When thinking about activities for this emotion, what does the dog love to do; who do they care most about? Some dogs gravitate toward a, favorite toy, or a favorite person. This dog might be attention seeking, have separation anxiety, bond too closely to one person, protective or human reactive. Any type of activity or game with favorite person is one that will be enjoyed.

- **Interactive toy play.** Games to see how dog and guardian interact. What is their relationship like?

- **Identifying games.** Games to find, object naming (as described under emotion of Lust above). What is dog responsive to, a favorite toy(s) or a favorite person?

- **On and off switch games.** impulse satisfying strategies that eventually leads to self satisfying strategies.

Panic – Games and problem-solving to change behavior

Panic includes separation anxiety and other anxiety behaviors that cause a dog to have "episodes" or "panic attacks". Separation anxiety occurs when pet guardian is away and their dog panics, howls, barks, destroys property and soils homes.

MRI studies have shown that physical pain and social pain share common cognitive and neural systems in the brain. Separation anxiety is considered a psychological problem according to Dr. Karen Overall, specialist in psychological illness in animals. An estimated 15 percent of all dogs suffer from a fear of separation. Interestingly, fifteen percent (15 %) of CED cases (out of over 700) are separation anxiety-related or a total of 105 cases.

The ethological fact that gentle handling of the young can stop their cries of separation, in part through the release of endorphins and oxytocin, but if left alone pups can suffer catastrophic 'psychic pain' and will often die

Games that are interactive, maintain interest and focus, and provide rewards that make staying alone fun are key elements.

One-eyed Jack, now happy to stay alone on his safety zone. In memory of Jack, who could stay home alone for long periods of time because he had activities to satisfy him, to keep him busy and to tire his mind. He became successful at self-soothing until the day he passed in his forever home. RIP sweet Jack.

Setting up an indoor "find it" course. This also helps to slowly and incrementally keep dog busy, while leaving the guardian at first turns back to dog, then later leaves the room and ideally leaves home for varying lengths of time. Leaving equals the good things flow, and soon the dog will be happy to stay alone. The key here is to "know your dog". Identify the appetitive motivators, such as type of food, toys, or other enrichment. The indoor find it course changes the habit of grabbing the keys, heading out the door, expecting the dog to subsist with nothing to work their mind (like closing you in a room with no books, crafts, tools etc.). Variety is the key here. And in the beginning short duration, working up to longer times away.

Jack, A Severe Case of Separation Anxiety

One-eyed Jack has quite a story to tell

Jack was found on the side of a road trembling, bloody and one eye gone. He was afraid. He had severe separation anxiety, jumping up and down and whining constantly and loudly were guardians to walk out the door for only a few seconds. He was a case of chronic stress (see YouTube reference video in Resource section).

Anxiety creates panic

The goal was to create new neural pathways and new habits for Jack.

"As soon as we start getting all the special treats ready, all he (Jack) can focus on is the food. We prep a Kong-filled with wet canned food, fill an Everlasting Fun Ball filled with chopped up Natural Balance pieces, and give him a dental stick chew," Erin W., Delaware said. "A few minutes later, Jack comes back downstairs and spends 10-20 minutes trying to get all the treats out of the ball and the Kong. When he gets it all or is ready to give up, he will either hop up on the couch or head back upstairs to sleep on the bed."

The ideal was changing what leaving looked like and starting to practice it slowly during Jack's CED.

"If both of us need to leave, we have one person leave the house first, usually out the back door, a few minutes earlier than the other. Then the other one gathers all his treats and leaves them out in the living room. Jack grabs the dental stick and runs off up the stairs while Ray or I (Erin) leave the house."

Jack needed the added help of anxiety medications. He took Trazadone (50mg in the morning and 25mg at night) and 25mg of Clomipramine at night. The Trazadone significantly reduced his anxiety in general and also increased his appetite, which helped him become a lot more distracted and motivated by treat hides.

Pathological anxiety, fear and compulsive neuroses are caused by abnormal brain processes. The balance of certain chemicals arising from under or overproduction is often disturbed. In serious cases of mental illness this can lead to a total collapse of the brain's chemical framework. In those cases, only medication can help. In Jack's case, along with a CED and behavior modification, medication was also necessary and several were tried.

The sensory cortex's job is to prevent an inappropriate response rather than to produce an appropriate one. There is a speedier process internally where data goes straight to the amygdala. In an emergency this rapid response could be a matter of life or death. LeDoux calls it The Difference Between The Quick and the Dead.

The fear system, according to Panksepp (2005, 2006), manifests in the midbrain and stays there and manifests fear whether there is or is not something to fear, perceived fear i.e. thunderstorms. This is where long-standing fears stay and are hardest to rehabilitate.

In Jack's case results were seen, "He stays on the couch or the bed for the rest of the day and usually doesn't even get up until one of us comes home. When we walk back in the door, he will come running to greet us, but there is rarely ever any whining or even jumping up at us. He'll run to say hi, then runs back over to his Kong to try to get the stuff that was stuck at the bottom, or he runs and gets a toy to play with."

Trust and safety exercises are best plus various activities and games such as: close-up and thinking games that do not involve a lot of movement or stress moving target games safety games, mat as safety zone, relax on a mat (ROAM), Dr. Karen Overall's relaxation protocol, and Susan Garrett's Crate Games, mild obstacle coursework, discovery and foraging games, such as object naming, find it, search, short hide and seek games

Play

Wally discovery pile. Four dogs, reactive to other dogs, play and learn. Top photo. Fearful Wally learns to build confidence through nose work activities. Today he has passed his first formal nose work class with flying colors. Bottom photo. Four fearful dogs learn interacting with each other is fun, builds confidence. Dogs learn from each other too and can help each other overcome fears.

Play is a dog's laboratory to real life. Here is where they practice their innate skills, such as chase, seeking, prey play and learn how objects, sounds respond. They learn what makes toys move, and how to socially interact with others, as well as how to respond to social cues and stimuli. They learn to problem solve, think and experience what works and what does not. And most importantly, play is a ton of fun building good stress, eustress.

The best way to help a dog learn to play is through playful activities; toys and alone games to discover if the dog is creative or not. It is the pet guardians responsibility to discover play the dog loves. Play also helps the dog build relationships with pet guardians and other dogs, and helps create strong bonds. The problem is that some dogs never learn to play, or do not have variety and are not mentally challenged in play. This type of dog will most likely display behavior problems.

In the CED, dogs are proofed for their noninteractive and interactive play skills. Ninety-percent of the dogs going through the CED did not know how to play alone, only 10-percent of the dogs could play alone, be creative in their play.

On the other hand, ninety-percent of dogs could play interactively with their pet guardians or caretakers, only 10- percent of the dogs did not want to, found it challenging, or were unsure what to do. Dogs who learn to play early and who play often have the least behavior problems.

Choosing mentally tiring activities to build relationships and create stronger bonds

When a dog has behavior issues, often it destroys the relationship and bond between that dog and those in the family. Anger, frustration, confusion is all a part of what the pet guardian goes through when the dog they have does not meet expectations. Observation activities can help to build or restore relationships and mend broken bonds. Here are some to try:

Observation activities. You can learn a lot about how a dog thinks that will help you to be a better teacher during behavior modification during a CED. Each dog is an individual and should be treated that way. If a dog confuses easily, watch for handling style of guardian, chunk steps down into easier to do pieces. If a dog is persistent and thinks fast, set them up for success by not allowing them to become bored increasing activity pieces of cycle.

Observation activities should show how a dog thinks or does not. Both are a choice. Are they a dog who needs smaller training sessions, gets frustrated easily, or simply cannot focus and gets confused? All these things should be very forefront in a CED and later a behavior modification process that focuses on the individual.

Here is one example of testing a dog's observation skills:

Cup Test

Goal: To sharpen senses, attention, focus and memory, all to make training easier and to get dog into a thinking state-of-mind.

Cup Test – foraging, building confidence. Here are three cup workouts, from How Dogs Think by Immanuel Birmelin.

Test one uses two cups, different shapes, and sizes. Dog should be sitting three feet away observing you. Put food under one of the cups, both are turned upside down. Give the find it or search cue.

Switch position of cups and increase distance of dog's observation point. Food is always under same cup. When the dog goes straight to the right cup, he has grasped the concept, so you can raise criteria. This is very much how all teaching should take place with dogs and instills observation skills in you, their teacher.

Test two uses five cups, one of which is the same one from test one and where the food will be hidden. Give find it or search cue.

Again, change position of cup, and make it harder by placing cups randomly around the room. Praise your dog for making the right decision. Stay with it until it becomes too easy or boring.

Test three. Line five cups in a row, but place food under a different cup. Give find it or search cue. Most dogs will head for the cup in the previous tests. This shows how a dog will respond to disappointment. Will they keep searching, be persistent? Will they just stand there confused or walk away?

In a CED there is no wrong or right, just observation and information. Other observation activities would include:

Recognition game. This dog is working on a symbol recognition activity during her CED. She approaches apprehensively, not sure if she should approach and get the food in the bowl labeled with a triangle. She also is reactive on approaching people, apprehensive, fearful. Her behavior modification program would take that into consideration to keep her successful.

Symbol Recognition, memory exercise

Clue Test, attentiveness, an example would be putting a ball on top of a cup (or anything as an added clue) and then blocking dog's view while changing cups (two cups are used).

Food is under cup with "clue", the ball. The ball represents where the treat is hidden. The difference is the exercise is more difficult as there is the addition of an object, a clue and the dog's view is blocked once the clue and food are placed. The clue is rearranged and then the dog is given the find it or search cue, as soon as the barrier comes down to reveal the "clue".

The questions to ask are, is the dog attentive? focused? Do they memorize where the food is? getting the clue?

Other tests might include:

Scenting, nose work, problem-solving to activate seeking system

Pointing at, dogs are one of the few animals that can respond to a finger point. This can help build relationships and allow the dog to pay attention to details.

Studies show that dogs comprehend human gestural communication in a way that other animal species do not. Pointing at and gazing at are two ways we can communicate to our dogs. It makes sense that while we are teaching a dog what our gestures mean, that we reciprocally learn what their gestures to us mean, such as a nose touch, a nudge, a paw lift, eye movements, body tension.

Naming objects, to create awareness, concentration, focus, thinking

Shell game, a common game everyone knows how to play, to test scent and ability to watch.

Color and Size for observation skills and memory

Logic activities, to create settings where dog must think about problem-solving, logically, how to get to something like food, a ball, Frisbee etc. For instance, if I leave one opening in a fence or one door open in the home, but toss a ball into a fenced area far away from that opening, or into a hallway that is blocked, the dog would must figure out logically that that opening leads to the area the ball is located. Spatial perception problems can be challenging and can be made more challenging using string and barriers. Concentration, work ethic, persistence are all analyzed. Shortest way in or out problems involving hiding a valued toy or food and dog has to figure out where opening is in house or outdoors in a fenced area or labyrinth and how to gain access.

A logic game used in the CED as a problem-solving activity:

The basket challenge

GOAL: To test how the dog thinks and responds to the environment.

My favorite logic activity is the basket challenge. This one is used consistently as a part of the mentally tiring activities in the CED, usually in day two or three.

Strips of cloth and treats are turned into a test of logic, from Biologist, Immanuel Birmelin's book "How Dogs Think", one of my favorite resources for mental workouts. This activity challenges reasoning skills and observational skills. Setting it up requires a see-through bicycle basket, fishing basket or box, or laundry basket.

Jack (human and dog reactive) and basket challenge Client, Steve Ayers made a basket out of a Pacific NW fishing basket, which Canine Transformations uses to this day. This is sheltie Jack, formerly human reactive using this fishing basket in a Confident Transformations class.

The dog must be able to look through whatever item you choose. It requires that the basket be weighted, so dog is not able to plow through it to get the food.

To start there is one strip of cloth. Food is placed on it at the end of the strip inside the box. Part of the cloth is sticking outside of the box. The dog must put two and two together to figure out the food is on the strip of cloth and if they pull the cloth, the food will come with it. You can make this test increasingly more difficult, by the addition of two, three and four cloths or covering the food on the cloth with a see-through container.

Observe that the dog walks around the box, looks in, possibly walks away to think about it but comes back quickly to solve the puzzle. Some dogs must think about it, and the pet guardian is instructed not to encourage, to let the dog think it through.

Some highly stressed dogs do not have the ability to solve problems, they are shut down, or extremely fearful, afraid of the objects, or do not have a good bond or relationship with their pet guardian.

What to look for when observing problem-solving activities

Dogs who can think through problems do well in behavior modification programs. Allowing the domesticated dog the opportunity to think is something dog pet guardians do not do regularly. If the dog walks away to think, the instruction is to let them. Give the dog a choice. If the dog is not allowed to think, the dog will get frustrated, or confused, or might quit altogether. If a dog is afraid, or cannot participate then that is information to carry forward to a behavior modification program once the CED ends.

Observe to see if the dog looks for the easy way out, or do they ponder the problem by watching another dog or person complete it. Do they think for themselves, or need some type of encouragement, or is encouragement too much for them and they shut down? How long does it take to solve the problem? It is a very key process of identification to help the individual be successful once a behavior modification program is implemented postCED.

What do mentally tiring activities reveal about a dog

Observing a dog's activities, how they approach a problem, and how they think can reveal their personality, identify clear stress or calming signals (signals a pet guardian might not have caught before and can now look for), and how their dog thinks or does not think.

Here are some examples of what mentally tiring activities can reveal about a dog:

Unreliable canine, as in the case of Harley the Pitbull (see Resource section for YouTube link)

Cognitive dysfunction or disorder, in older dogs the term is dysfunction and is a disease prevalent in dogs that exhibit symptoms of dementia or Alzheimer's disease shown in humans. It can start as early as 11- years-old and show up behaviorally with difficulties in spatial orientation, memory problems, and difficulty in recognizing and reacting to human family members, or focal difficulties.

- Short sessions are better canine
- Irritable canine, usually means health issues of some type
- PTSD (post traumatic stress) canine
- Easy way is better canine
- Meticulous or routine-oriented canine

I have to think about it or I might need to avoid this canine, as in the case of Chai, mixed breed (see Resource section for YouTube link) or it is going to take time and patience dog – Chai avoids the fearful Canine OR any combination of the above behavior

All can be analyzed just by observing how a dog solves a problem. All have impact on how a behavior modification program should be developed for the individual. The CED Final Analysis will create a customized system to assure progress is made with each dog based on personality, individualized issues and how to solve them.

Chapter 9

Communication Is Two-Way

"Pay attention to the individual in front of you." - Susan Friedman

During the CED, how pet guardians are interacting with their dog will come forward, as well as how the dog is responding to those interactions.

The way a dog communicates alters the circuitry of their brain. On the flip side, the way a dog is communicated 'to' by family members (or others, including family pets, strange dogs and strange people) also alters the circuitry of their brain. Mindful communication equals transformation and behavior change.

Communication is a two-way process and the CED allows the pet guardian to form a communication with their dog resulting in an increase of understanding, a better relationship, and a stronger bond. In CED after CED, it was evident there were specific behavior insights coming to the forefront, and learning between pet guardian, trainer and dog became all important in the implementation of a successful behavior modification program.

Communication takes place between two animals when an observer can detect predictable changes in the behavior of one of them in response to signals from the other (Wilson, 1975). In this sense, communication would include an extensive range of behaviors, which are often emitted by animals in their daily lives to solve different problems like searching for food, mates, territory, and in some species, playing, cooperating etc.

Experimental learning psychology defines communication as a set of chained responses, where the signals act as discriminative stimuli that prompt the receiver to perform a certain response. This behavior, as a consequence, leads to a reward for one or both animals (Skinner 1953).

Clear communication and allowing a dog to make choices increases confidence. In teaching dogs, we expect them to listen to us and learn, but often it is unclear whether we are listening to them or not. Communication is a two-way interaction, not a one-sided lecture.

Five ways to better communicate with a canine companion:

1. **Learn to read canine body language.** Dogs are communicating through their body language all the time, from ear position, to eye flicks, to how they wag their tail.

2. **Keep cues easy to understand.** This provides clarity. One word cues are best in the beginning, such as sit versus sit down, which will be confusing. What do you mean? To sit, or to lie down?

3. **Learn to use a clicker and/or a marker word or other sound or body cue.** The consistency of the sound or body cue allows the dog to know when they have done something right that warrants a food reward. This will increase the behavior wanted. The sound provides a bridge of communication between species, a bridge of understanding.

4. **Reward the dog for what they are doing RIGHT**, instead of worrying about what they are doing WRONG. The right behavior will increase, strengthen. The bad behavior will diminish and extinguish.

5. **Take the time to learn to use a collar, leash, harness in a gentle and communicative manner.** Equipment should kindly represent what you want the dog to do, and influence behavior in a fear free manner.

We can choose to learn to communicate through the use of various tools, communication bridges, using proper leading tools and teaching through luring, shaping, capturing, social modeling and more. Dogs are adept at reading body language and so by positively using our eyes, voice tone, breathing rate, posture we can capture and keep their attention. As a result, they will choose to be with us willingly and joyfully.

Giving choices is simple and part of the communication process, such as allowing a dog to make a choice on whether they want to meet a person or not, want to play with a dog or not, want to sit in a puddle of water or not.

Everyday dogs are faced with choices and helping them make good choices, good decisions helps them to trust, to feel safe and to be more confident. Allowing a dog the right to walk away to think while solving a problem is okay, and so is allowing a fearful dog to choose to walk away or back away from something scary.

Choosing a squeaky toy over a tug toy, or other combination is choice that shows what the dog prefers. Knowing they can choose gives them confidence in their environment. Dogs can make great positive choices based on how we communicate with them, what reinforcements are used, and how teaching is broken down into easy to learn increments. The more information received about how a dog thinks during a CED, the more successful the resulting behavior modification program can be to help solve challenges.

Behavior insights of CED

How does a CED help develop insights into behavior? A CED:

1. gets to the CORE of the behavior

2. builds knowledge of the canine, their environment, their family

3. provides deeper insights so behavior can change effectively, progressively

4. creates a final analysis as the basis for a behavior modification and skills deficits process

5. can help identify health issues and make it clear if other professionals need to be brought into the process

What do the dog's pet guardian and trainer learn in the CED process? They learn:

1. how the dog interacts with its environment

2. about the pet guardian dog bond and relationship

3. how the dog processes information

4. how dog may respond in real life contexts

5. why the dog is responding to triggers

6. of possible health issues allowing the trainer to immediately recommend a veterinarian, veterinarian behaviorist, or other specialist

All the above have a direct impact on the behavior modification program and how the dog will begin to process the information so trainer and pet guardian can help them overcome their challenges. The CED becomes more than just a stress release process, but a chance to observe, analyze and be a teaching tool, an application to a solid behavior modification journey to change emotional responses.

How will trainer communicate CED process with pet guardian? How does it fit this into a training and behavior process?

The CED is a hands-on process complete with custom plans, daily analysis and final analysis dependent on detailed observations. There are several ways to implement the CED.

1. board and train keeping detailed notes, compiling scrapbooks for the pet guardian, and creating a final analysis of next steps that becomes the behavior modification program

2. phone consults, but please note trainers are always very hands on

3. remote implementation through digital photographs, video and skype or facetime. Since there is no training during a CED, implementing and viewing visuals long distance is feasible. It is all about releasing stress.

4. local clients can do CED without coming to the trainer, going to a facility, but right in their home with trainer close and next steps able to occur post-CED through the final analysis

Patterns should jump out during a CED. For best CED results, it is best completed as a team effort, with trainer and pet guardian working over 72 hours, versus something your client does on their own. Now that said, if pet guardians wishes to follow the cycle and examples given in this book, they can, however not being a professional means the analysis will be incomplete. The pet guardian will not see what a trained eye can. It is always best for challenging dogs to consult with a force free professional, one who will have the dog's and guardian's best interests at heart. The added benefit for the trainer is CED also gives important feedback about the pet guardian and how they interact with their dog. It can make the difference between a successful or unsuccessful behavior modification program.

How will pet guardian participate with the process?

The pet guardian is the best choice to work with the dog, as a bonding process goes on during the CED. It is priceless for eroded relationships due to behavior challenges. A rescue or shelter personnel, or foster, or trainer can also do a CED, but the dog will bond to the one implementing the process. The process is done as follows.

1. over three days, a full 72 hours, no less

2. based on behavior seen outwardly

3. provides a generalized preparation list of items

4. client does process as outlined, in order given

5. a client can just do the cycle themselves, but a trainer adds a dimension that cannot be achieved by doing the process alone, especially where challenging dogs are involved, where health issues might be present, and where analysis to help next steps would be vital

What it all means can be simply pulled out as it is all about stress release and mood changes, it is about faster progress because the dog can learn better, faster, retain more and more successfully follow a behavior modification and skills applications process. Results can be long-lasting.

The CED builds good stress chemicals (eustress) both without medication or in conjunction with medication on a case by case basis.

What about the standard way of gathering information through intake forms and functional assessments?

Behavior modification based on an intake form and functional assessment are fine, but are they enough?

The intake form is based on the client's opinion of the situation and a functional assessment is a living document, but created initially in a 1.5 to 2-hour trainer analysis of the situation, but is it enough?

Does it show how the dog thinks, exactly why the dog is responding to triggers or stimuli? The results and observations of the CED do the following to add to the intake form, and the functional assessment. The CED is also a living document for the course of the dog's therapy and rehabilitation from a team point of view. The CED:

1. sets dog up for success

2. builds a better relationship between dog and pet guardian

3. releases stress through deep sleep

4. makes dog focus on process

5. is low stress, force free and fun

6. relationship is revived, reactivity is diminished, it opens the mind, creates new neural pathways

7. the dogs needs are met allowing keen observations to be done, where the dog within comes out

8. emphasis and importance is on deep sleep, tiring mental activity and problem-solving

9. shows other ways to exercise, to keep minds sharp and reactions low to zero

10. shows once stress is released focus can be on behavior modification and skills deficits

11. explains how stress release means the dog can learn faster, better and retain longer

12. decreases time needed to changing behavior because stress isn't main issue

13. teaches pet guardian to learn positively about their dog and how to best work with them

14. teaches trainers how to best work with pet guardians and their dog as a team

15. reveals the dog within so a proper team of professionals can be established to work through issues, for instance a canine nutritionist, veterinarian, veterinarian behaviorist, physical therapist, groomer, dog walker, and whatever it takes to resolve and relieve behavior issues

It is a process customized to each individual situation and home environment and is why this book is so hard to write. TThere are no recipes in working with challenging dogs, each individual must be observed as to who they are and how they think.

Chapter 10

Starting line and What To Do AFTER CED

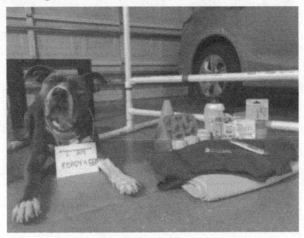

Bridget readies for her CED

"CED and working with Bridget has opened my eyes into a dog's potential, in general. They are amazing creatures but we don't take advantage of that, I mean the 'common' people. Dogs are so capable of learning. If people could see that and be less lazy and truly work with them probably there would be less surrendering of pets in shelters and animal abuse penalties would be stricter." (RIP Bridget, Jan 2021, cancer)
- Katia Leon, North Carolina

It starts with a preparation list (chapter 4). Most items will be readily available in the home.

The 72-hours is a systematic checklist of action items. Pet guardian checks off each item as they move through the CED. The first goal, in day one is complete, willing relaxation, leading to a full eight-hours of uninterrupted sleep. Pet guardians MUST commit to taking time with their dogs for three full days with zero distractions.

A modest fee can and should be charged to implement a CED by the trainer. It is as important as a private session and will take approximately

20 hours of a trainer's analysis over a three-day period. It can also be part of the charge, if local, of a functional assessment. This should be paid one week prior to start of CED. The CED requires intense focus and learning about the individual challenged by behavioral issues and can be the beginning that changes the outcome. It is and should be a service offered to solve behavior problems. Behavior problems always start with high stress levels, acute or chronic. Stress matters.

Two company policy forms should be signed and filled out, a photo, video, comment permission form and a liability form specific to the CED (see Appendix for samples). These should be returned before implementing the CED. Implementing a CED should be taken as seriously as implementing a behavior modification program, as it helps and should be a part of a results-oriented outcome.

A step-by-step day one is customized according to behavioral issue and sent two day priors to start point; while days two and three are customized to the individual based day one. These arrive, along with day's analysis at the end of days two and three.

How do you customize the first day of the CED to behavioral issue?

First, identify the dog's triggers. This should have been done through the intake form and a functional analysis completed for a trainer's local clients. Remote clients and trainer work, will most likely include another trainer locally who will complete a functional assessment. What is being seen?

- Intrahousehold aggression – multi-dog household fighting
- Interhousehold aggression – dog to dog reactivity or aggression
- Reactive to or fear of people
- Sensitivity to objects or sounds
- Predatory behavior or predatory drift
- Bite history
- Hyperactivity
- Combination of above

Basic day one plus behavior additions

There is a basic day one format, but depending on the main behavior challenge, additions can be made as follows.

The changes to day one would be subtle but in a multi-dog household fighting situation, you might add one exercise a day that includes a relaxed, treat-oriented process where two dogs can have a positive experience with each other. Every time they are together good things happen or they are not together. This exercise could be added in the physical stimulation piece of the cycle (see how to section).

If a dog is sensitive to other dog's barking, or the sound of tags, the CED might be a good place to start a very low-level desensitization to those sounds. Add as a sensory piece to the cycle. (see How To section, Chapter 11)

Reactivity or fear of people or those with bite histories an easy addition to the CED day one might include things like teaching a surprise cue, or a proper meet and greet protocol with familiar people (the pet guardians), or an exercise in targeting and touching a palm of the hand, all as a part of or in addition to the problem-solving activity piece in the CED cycle (see how to section).

The addition of appropriate play items, such as a flirt pole, an automatic tennis ball machine, a treat and train exercise in a toy play segment of the cycle could benefit those with chase or predatory instincts or the hyperactive dog, the one who has trouble settling. The addition of multiple problem-solving activities, toy play, physical stimulation would be satisfying and mentally tiring helping further the goal of the CED, deep sleep.

By the end of day one, through comments, video reviews, digitals, the stage will be set for customizing day two of the CED. While there is a basic systematic format, customizing is in the simplicity of the process with attention to patterns seen in day one to create the additions to and customization of day two. For example, a pet guardian may not have done an exercise a clue to add it into the next day in the proper order. A dog may not be able to relax, so adding more mentally tiring activity in day two would help. So you would add additional puzzle pieces to the cycle in the toy category, the physical stimulation category or the problem-solving category OR all the above. Add as many as needed. A Belgian Malinois may need more activity than an English Bulldog, for instance. The goal is always deep sleep during a CED. If a dog is able to relax, calm and sleep in the first day, then you'd want to increase the time in the relaxation periods as appropriate.

The patterns, comments, video reviews, digitals will by now have provided enough information for the last day, where relaxation, calm, deep sleep occurs and sticking to the exact CED cycle formula is rarely an issue by day three.

What happens after a CED is completed

There will be questions to answer at the end of day three. From this point is where the trainer will pull together what was learned into a continuing behavioral plan and skills training, a final analysis. Important and life-changing information about the dog and the client will be learned through the completion of the CED. If you are a pet guardian reading this book, it is important you keep detailed notes, make comments, take video and digitals so that if you start work with a trainer you can pass this along, and more importantly that you learn about your dog objectively, which is awfully hard to do with our own dogs. Work with a CED certified trainer or contact author, Diane Garrod.

Chronically stressed dogs may show up in about 10% of the cases a trainer sees. It simply means this dog needs additional days of relaxation and deep sleep, continuance of the CED, from 5 to 21 days. Severe case dogs may need two CEDs and regular maintenance CEDs of one or two days is advised quarterly, before a stressful event, or after a stressful event. Dog pet guardians would be wise to continue a day-long CED throughout the dog's lifetime for the pure enjoyment of it and a relationship and bond building exercise for all involved. However, most dogs and pet guardians have needed no more than two CEDs in extreme cases of chronic stress. The vast majority (90%) needed only one CED.

What the pet guardian will learn about the dog is:

- how the dog relaxes
- do they have ability to focus
- does dog have ability to enjoy their food
- how they deal with boredom or repetition
- what their stress signals are
- what dog's optimal time of day is when they are most active
- to pay attention to details to include movement, hot or cold spots, painful areas, stomach issues, waste consistency, color and content and if other professionals need to be added to help with dog's behavior modification

After the CED is completed the cycle in Chapter five (The Right Combination) becomes the Dog's Ideal Day to keep stress in normal levels and build eustress on a daily basis.

The Keys to A Dog's Ideal Day

The keys to a dog's ideal day has specific elements. The CED research has shown that what releases stress can also be described as keys to a dog's ideal day. Following a certain set of guidelines, in effect, keeps stress in the good to normal ranges, while keeping the building of harmful stress, the stress that can cause behavior and health issues, minimal. Some of the elements that are key to a dog's ideal day may surprise you.

First, relaxation/sleep comprises 50% of a dog's ideal day, with 20% sensory or toy play, 20% enrichment and problem-solving and 10% physical stimulation and exercise.

Like a combination to a safe, the exact numbers open to reveal the contents of the dog's ideal day in the cycle illustration, Chapter five (The Right Combination). In a dog's life, the combination to their ideal day opens their world, and creates a stronger bond and relationship with their humans, enriching their lives. It Is worth the effort to get that combination right for the dog you have or for client dogs.

Let's look at the definition of ideal? From the Merriam-Webster dictionary, it is defined in four ways:

1. Existing as an archetypal (very typical of a certain kind of person or thing) idea

2. Existing as a mental image or in a fancy or imagination only, broadly; lacking practicality; relating to or constituting mental images, ideas or conceptions

3. Of, relating to, or embodying an ideal, ideal beauty for instance; conforming exactly to an ideal, law or standard, perfect

4. Of or relating to philosophical idealism

Applying one word, ideal means perfect, such as an ideal spot, ideal vacation or ideal opportunity, perfect in every way. In application, a dog's ideal day would be their perfect day. As we all know, our own lives aren't ideal, or perfect, so knowing what comprises an ideal day is the key to being as close as possible to implementing those keys. Some days will not be ideal, but they can still be enriching. By that standard, a dog's ideal day is then what is satisfying, what is enriching. Each person's idea of their dog's ideal day can be quite different and often depends on lifestyle.

Let's look at what is NOT ideal – too much of anything, or not enough of anything; too much exercise, too much sleep; not enough environmental enrichment, not enough interaction and bonding. Somewhere in between the ideal and the not so ideal is a great guide to how a dog's day can keep stress levels minimal, keep them satisfied and content, and keep behavior problems minimal. Those comprise the keys to an ideal day.

When I asked several people what their dog's ideal day is, the answers I got were:

*   no triggers,

- a special food or eating all day,
- nose work, find it and other sniffing games,
- a car trip,
- a trip to the park,
- hunting,
- playing in the water and swimming,
- naps,
- a game of fetch,
- trick or other training,
- play dates,
- cuddles,
- a hike somewhere special,
- laying or playing in the sand,
- enrichment walk,
- specialized work (i.e. therapy dog, agility),
- chews,
- working on food toys and squeaky toys,
- running off lead, time with pet guardian,
- getting brushed,
- outdoor enrichment,
- game of tug,
- special outings,
- unlimited treats and attention,
- basic training,
- body awareness exercises, and
- scavenging

This is a great and lengthy list, but lacking a systematic format or ideal. Where does one start? Each dog, each human is slightly different showing diversity, lifestyle and various environments and interests. All are wonderful, but what is the right combination that makes for an ideal day, an enriched day and keeps stress minimal and satisfaction optimal bringing all the loose ends together postCED?

Allowing for a dog's unique qualities, personality, age, breed will have a significant impact on what constitutes their ideal day. The career, job, personality, expectations, ideals of the pet guardian will also have a significant impact. Even with these variables, working within the keys to a dog's ideal day (for all dogs) can organize the day, provide pet guardian with peace of mind, and help their dog be a better companion with minimal issues.

It's the little things that make a difference. Your dog is giving you clues all the time by being excited to go on a walk, or just out somewhere with you, or grabbing a favorite toy, or showing off what they know, or sleeping where they can find a restful day or night. And they give you clues when they are not getting what they need like over-barking, becoming hyper-aroused, destroying, digging, chasing prey, ignoring you, refusing to eat and escaping to have adventures of their own.

To curb, prevent and work through behavior problems a dog's day should be more than average. Let's look at six areas that formulate a dog's ideal day.

Everything revolves around the environment. One cycle per day in the cycle would be ideal (see Chapter five), however, noting where you left off, and starting in next segment, when you can is also being ideal. In stress release, this cycle would be repeated two to three times per day over a 72-hour period. Starting at the top of the circle is the provision of the best nutrition for the individual, so health can be optimal. Evaluating biologics, such as waste is an effortless way for a companion dog guardian to know when their dog is ill. The other elements rotate clockwise starting with an after eating digestion relaxation period of 10 to 20 minutes and any exercise period would allow for a 20-minute minimum relaxation before eating or until respiration comes down.

Relaxation periods throughout the day

Dogs need 12 to 14 hours of sleep daily (8 hours at night), so two to four hours during the day. According to the National Sleep Foundation (www.sleep.org) about 10 percent of a dog's sleep is REM. The result is that they need more total sleep in order to log enough of the restorative kind of REM they need. Puppies, who expend a lot of energy exploring and learning may need as much as 18 to 20 hours. Dogs often spend 50 percent of the day sleeping, 30 percent lying around awake, and just 20 percent being active.

The relaxation periods in a dog's ideal day cycle can be 20 minutes to one hour or more in length and follow activity periods, which studies show are important to memory and learning in dogs. Recently a team of researchers in Budapest conducted a study of sleep and memory in dogs. The goal was to evaluate the effects of what a dog does after a training session and his ability to retain what he learned during the session. The study included two phases and involved a group of volunteer pet dogs and their owners. The first phase used an electroencephalogram (EEG) to measure the dogs' brain electrical activity after a training session in which they learned a task. The second phase looked at the impact of different types of post-learning activities (such as napping) on the dogs' memory consolidation, both short- and long-term.

Daily Sensory Activities or Toys/Games

While a dog's brain is only one-tenth the size of a human brain, the portion controlling smell is 40 times larger than in humans. According to the Alabama Cooperative Extension System (ACES), a dog's sense of smell is about 1,000 times keener than that of their two-legged companions. As a dog inhales a scent, it settles into his spacious nasal cavity, which is divided into two chambers and, ACES reports, is home to more than 220 million olfactory receptors (humans have a measly 5 million). Looking at just a dog's nose in this way shows how important sensory activities are to them.

A terrific book to go into depth on the importance of a dog's nose, of sniffing is "Being a Dog" by Alexandra Horowitz.

The rest of the senses need exercising too, taste through tasty rewards and nutritional meals, hearing various sounds, and mindful touch to form a positive connection.

Sensory activities would include:

1. foraging for meals,

2. sniffing on an awareness walk, allowing a dog to be a dog

3. find it games,

4. aroma therapy,

5. aromatic sensory gardens to explore (http://www.yourdog.co.uk/ Dog-Health-and-Care/can-i-create-a-sensory-garden-for-my-dog.html)

6. warm towel to relieve muscle tension,

7. mindful touch like Tellington Touch (www.tellingtontouch.com) or animal massage

Picking one sensory activity in the morning before leaving for work, or letting a dog play with favorite toys or searching for their breakfast in games can go a long way to satisfying what they need prior to starting a work day.

Here are ten ways to use toys and intelligence games to mentally tire the dog's brain.

1. Foraging or intelligence toys, something the dog needs to work at to solve

2. Hiding toys, balls, intelligence games outdoors to find

3. Opening the toy box and letting dog(s) pick their favorites to play

4. DIY toys, such as a muffin tin filled with balls and treats, towel rolls or bottles as food finds, a taped-up box to work at to get toys and rewards

5. Toys that talk, roll, interact and smart toys the dog must learn to solve. These can get high tech such as, Go Bone – adding a little motion to your dog's life – https://mygobone. com/?v=7516fd43adaa

6. Before leaving for work, set up a find it course of safe activities, like hidden, filled Kong

7. Set up calming aids such as adaptil diffusers, aromas such as lavender, and audible sounds like a radio or TV on timer, all to relax and provide variety in a dog's day

8. There are 1001 DIY ideas on Pinterest. Here are my Pinterest boards to get started https://www.pinterest.com/dgarrod3/

9. Set up pre-desensitized mats to signal relaxation plus a game or two nearby hidden under a towel or blanket to work on later

10. Snuffle Mats can be bought or made – how to make or buy http:// pamsdogtraining.com/snuffle-mats-are-now-for-sale/ or https:// www.etsy.com/uk/listing/247178407/dog-snuffle-mat-treat-puzzle-large (photo)

Exercise or Physical Stimulation and Movement

Dogs need exercise for physical fitness, but exercise is not all they need. Exercise can come in many forms, one is housecersize (setting up obstacle courses around the house and yard, on leash yard walks, filling a backpack of fun dispersing items like tug toys, various types of balls, a flirt pole and more), or body movements through K9 Conditioning (www.fitpaws.com), parkour (www.dogparkour.org), dog sports, walks or jog, off lead runs, sprinting activities like fetch. Pick one. Vary what is done daily. These work different muscles.

Mentally tiring problem-solving

Dogs who problem-solve cope better and become thinking dogs. Problem-solving is quite different from toy play, intelligence toys, enrichment in that it requires a dog think through a problem dealing with finding, connectivity, making decisions, following clues and more. A favorite book, which has a daily mental workout is "How Dogs Think" by Immanuel Birmelin, https://www.amazon.com/How-Dogs-Think-Beautiful-Relationship/dp/0760786658.

Multiple Dogs

An ideal day for multiple dogs can be challenging and while the format stays the same, who does it and when is different. I have two dogs and I like to rotate who does what and where in the cycle. Providing for one-on-one time with guardian is important as well as time together. Providing safe zones and areas of relaxation for everyone is important.

Working Guardian – Away from home eight hours

This is not good for puppies or highly active adolescent dogs, but making provisions for pet sitting in the home, or someone coming in to spend time with a dog can prevent behavior issues from developing. Most dogs will be content sleeping most of the time a person is away from home, but puppies, adolescents, and many highly energetic breeds need more.

Burning off energy is important in a dog's ideal day and so the working guardian needs to start their dog's day with a 30 to 60-minute walk. Starting the dog's ideal day cycle each morning at the physical stimulation/exercise/training level will benefit everyone. Ideally, if someone trusted could come in to walk dog(s), that would allow for problem-solving, nutrition, digestion relaxation, and sensory or toys in the evening as all wind down.

High tech solutions could include, even for those that do not spend a lot of time away or have home businesses, supervise dog via an indoor security camera or set-up video chat over Skype. Set up an account, enable auto-answer, and leave home computer on in a strategic area of the home. Why? This would allow you to let dog(s) hear the voice of one they love and trust throughout the day.

To keep dog busy and prevent boredom at home, if they are trusted to stay outside of their crate, set up a foraging course before leaving. Cups spread out around the house with treats underneath, or a favorite ball, or a stuffed Kong can provide mentally tiring activity. Put treats s in a Kong or hide treat dispensing toys, but make sure they are safe and have no small parts. Put out chews, toys that dog can interact, such as those that spin or talk or move.

The Clever Pet, https://clever.pet/, interactive feeding game is also a great tool evaluated in the September 2017 issue of Barks from the Guild. It is a training process of shaping by successive approximations and connects to WIFI. Dog must figure out which light pad sequence release a reward. There are several levels according to the article.

What is the key? What does it look like? Look at providing for your dog's day as an adventure. The key is always right in front of you. How fun or boring you make it is totally up to you, what adventures you provide in the way of enrichment, outings, is up to you. Your dog will happily follow your lead.

Looking online for a dog's ideal will most likely reveal an incomplete picture or one that makes excuses for why a dog doesn't have an ideal day or fit into our very busy lives. Some talk about developing a routine, taking walks for exercising Fido, a block of time for training, fitting a dog into your schedule. Really though, what would that ideal be from a dog's point of view, and would it fit into our time schedule or would it just happen naturally and openly.

Take a moment for yourself and your dog today. Get some ideal day elements in place, no matter your lifestyle and watch your dog thrive like never before.

The key is to offer the items above to your dog every day. If you look at the chart and leave off in one segment, mark it with a magnet, then you can just come back to the next segment and move forward systematically. Even if you don't cover all the elements comprising a dog's ideal day, you will be giving them the attention, enrichment, mentally tiring activity, exercise and rest they need consistently to keep problems minimal and enjoyment at a maximum. A true companion is a joy, whether human or canine.

The next move after the CED with your dog will make a significant impact on their ideal day. Set them up for success with 50% relax periods following activity and eating; 20% sensory or to play; 20% problem-solving and 10% physical stimulation and exercise. In an eight-hour day, a dog would relax/sleep four hours (one-hour or more between activities); problem-solve 1.5 hours (not all at once); do sensory activities or toy play 1.5 hours (not all at once) and have physical exercise/physical stimulation for one hour per day. It's the little things that make a difference!

Now let's look at the step-by-step, Chapter 11.

Chapter 11 How To Divider

Canine Emotional Detox

Stress release for the challenging dog

Illustration by Carol Byrnes, Diamonds in the Ruff, Spokane, WA depicting author and Chancellor (April 3, 2004 to January 24, 2015) working the process together on beautiful Whidbey Island in Puget Sound, but more importantly depicting that a pet guardian is the catalyst to their dog to release stress so the whole behavior modification process progresses with results. It is a journey. Chancellor is the reason the CED exists.

How to do a canine emotional detox (CED)

Trainer's Manual

The CED is:

- structured, specific on what to do and when

- safe, and promotes relaxation, sleep

- builds trust between the one doing the CED and the dog

- makes it easier to develop a behavior modification process and skills applications program because you are looking at patterns appearing within the CED that meet the needs of the individual.

You aren't guessing or applying this or that or defaulting to one technique that has worked in the past , you know.

In preparing to get started with a CED, it is important to remember that you are dealing with an individual and that while you have a plan, a right combination protocol, there is no recipe or magic. The individual's behavior(s), breed, personality, and their pet guardians will drive the stress release process. A trainer brings an objective eye to every case that a pet guardian might not have when it comes to their own dog and challenging behaviors. If you are a pet guardian, remember, it is always wise to work with a force free behavior consultant/trainer, veterinarian behaviorist. It is money well spent and will help understand your dog like never before.

It is a process customized to each individual situation and home environment.

The Preparation List

It starts with a checklist of action items. The pet guardian, shelter worker, trainer, board/train etc. check off each item as they move through the CED. The first goal, first day is complete relaxation and calm, leading to a full eight-hours of uninterrupted sleep. The pet guardian MUST commit to taking time with their dogs for three full days striving for zero distractions. See Chapter Four for preparation checklist basics.

Function of the days

The first day is customized to behavioral issue, while days 2 and 3 are customized to the individual seen in day one's process. There will be questions to answer at the end, a final question series, but observation comments and questions being answered by client are scattered throughout the three days. From this point is where the trainer will incorporate what was learned into a continuing behavioral plan and skills training. Important and often life- changing information about the dog and the client will be learned through the completion of the CED.

Understand that severe case dogs, those who are chronically stressed, may need two CEDs (second one a month apart or if possible, a continuous CED until goals are achieved). Maintenance CEDS done quarterly of one or two days are sufficient thereafter at times of increased stress. The CED will show:

- how the dog relaxes
- ability to focus
- satiation and enjoyment of food
- ability to withstand boredom or repetition

How to pull it all together

From hiding, to engaging

Information Gathering

Use this section as a workbook.

The four information gathering elements of a CED that make it different from other stress release processes are:

1. Client comments, which are the golden nugget, and often the key to changing behavior and understanding the relationship between dog and dog pet guardian.

2. Discovering patterns within the CED, compiled from observation, review of video, digitals, and comments. Discovering patterns can help save a dogs life.

3. Final Analysis pulls it all together after a 72-hour period of CED.

4. Final Analysis becomes the initial behavior modification program customized to the individual (or a support document to the behavior modification process) and is attentive to what ongoing stress release means to that individual.

If you are a trainer or pet professional, before implementing the CED, start here:

Intake Form

Gather information through an intake form just as you would for a private client. Even if you are a pet guardian, fill out the intake form prior to doing a CED with your dog. You will have that information to give to your trainer and it will clear your mind to focus on the dog and not to assume. Intake form example is in the Appendix Section.

Remember, the intake form is from the pet guardian's point of view. It can be informational and provide insights, but it is not objective. For the pet guardian, it will help focus your thoughts, identify triggers and when the behavior began, focus on what you are trying to change and to write the known facts/history down.

Trainers and behavior professionals should pay special attention to the pet guardian's three behavior priorities, as well as age of dog, breed or mix of, current diet, health issues, and current environment description (people, other animals, physical environment, how they spend their time, where dog exercises, relaxes, plays, and eats). This all helps define day one of the CED, which is compiled according to the cycle, of course, but also according to behavior and what you've defined in the intake form and functional assessment (if this is a local client).

Functional Assessment

A functional assessment should be completed for local clients. It is from perspective of trainer and will be important for information. A CED can be provided as a part of the cost of the functional assessment.

Important Forms

A permission form for use of comments, video, digitals should be filled out and signed and a liability form pertinent to CED. These forms are and should be company policy. Examples are in Appendix section.

Schedule three consecutive days

Schedule days and put them into calendar just as you would a private session.

Preparation List

This list has been discussed in Chapter Four and above. It should be sent one week prior to day one. Send forms in list above along with the preparation list.

Day one step-by-step preparation details

Examples of Day One behavior considerations:

Human or dog-dog reactivity or aggression means a complete stress vacation and rest from triggers. The environment must be set up to avoid any triggers that would be counterproductive to a stress release process. It would be counterproductive to start to release stress and then have a reaction to totally counteract the process. Remember, you are releasing stress, not creating it.

Separation anxiety case means adding elements to start work within the cycle of the process such as Roger Abrantes "Home Alone" or Malena DeMartini-Price's "Treating Separation Anxiety in Dogs". Pieces described in these books can be added as physical stimulation exercises, or even games elements. Of course, since being left alone can be stressful, it would start at seconds at first such as a find it game.

Over-barking means distraction must be kept to a minimum by closing blinds, changing how dog interacts with environment, even changing where dog is allowed in house during the process.

Sound sensitivities means keeping levels low and/or having a high rate of reinforcement in place. In a CED, sound can be worked with at low levels (i.e. a bark CD for instance) and a high reward system as an added exercise. This takes a certain skill to implement so make sure you know what you are doing, as the goal is stress release. If dog is local, do a functional analysis (of 1.5 to 2 hours) prior to implementing a CED. The CED becomes an extension of the functional analysis.

Detailed video, digitals, and comments

Video and/or digital photos during all steps, including sleep, is critical to the process and proper observation, analysis and pattern findings.

Compile Day One Example A Tale of Two Dogs – Mornings of two different dogs

As you go through this example to teach you how to compile day one of the CED, compare it to the cycle found in Chapter Five. Making a copy as a visual will help as you read through. It will start you thinking about how to structure the case for maximum effectiveness for the individual and their behavior issue(s). The right combination (Chapter Five) of elements is key to successful stress relief. Text in bold indicate differences in the two dog's days.

Jersey   Max

Jersey's Day One Morning Example
Female –January 2013 Dog, Reactivity, Fear and worry/Anxiety

- BEFORE BREAKFAST – potty, evaluate poo.
- BREAKFAST
- 20 M DIGESTION RELAXATION

- SENSORY ACTIVITY – WARMTH
- 1 HOUR RELAXATION
- NON-INTERACTIVE PLAY 15M
- 1 HOUR RELAXATION – no distractions – music
- ALONE TIME
- PROBLEM SOLVING – Color Recognition
- COMPLETED CYCLE 1 – lunch

Max's Day One Morning Example
Male– Max – February 2012 – Anxiety, Dog Reactive

- BEFORE BREAKFAST – potty, evaluate poo and do Ttouch and Belly Lift
- BREAKFAST
- 20 M DIGESTION RELAXATION
- **NON-INTERACTIVE PLAY – 15 M**
- RELAXATION – 1 HOUR
- ALONE TIME RELAXATION – 1 HOUR
- PROBLEM SOLVING – Color Recognition
- RELAXATION – 1 HOUR
- COMPLETED CYCLE 1– Lunch

In the two cases above, you are seeing a slight difference in the before breakfast piece. If a dog has digestive issues, as seen in the intake form with Max, ttouch and a belly lift (see How To on next page) are recommended prior to breakfast to help relax the stomach and help with digestion. Ttouch or Tellington Touch (www.tellingtontouch.com) is a technique of circular touches, lifts and strokes to relax a dog. The first relaxation period after breakfast is always a 20M rest period (see Chapter Six – The Dog Within as to why).

How to do a belly lift

Hold ends of an ace bandage with both hands, as seen in photo below. Make sure hands move up and down parallel (not at angles) for a count of 6 seconds up, and down 6 seconds. Motion should be smooth and slow. If is not an ace bandage available, interlock fingers under belly, or use a towel and lift. This continues to help with digestion and calms the dog. If it doesn't calm the dog, dog tries to bolt, or looks back, it could indicate stomach distress, which would be important observation to note. Dogs can have stomach aches causing pain and making them irritable.

Belly lifts example. This Great Dane, Bacon, loved the belly lift . He had chronic fecal incontinence and eventually had to be put to sleep because of severe health issues. He had his detox just prior (the final detox) and felt better than he'd ever felt in his lifetime. Bacon's behavior was that he had attacked another dog on a walk after being rescued.

Questions

The questions asked below, should be a part of the step-by-step hand-out to the pet guardian, so they can answer them after each section is completed (the sample day one is handout ready in the Appendix). Tweaks may be needed before presenting it to the pet guardian to customize to the dog going through the CED.

Questions to answer after breakfast meal to provide more observation and information gathering. The example uses *she* as pronoun and should be changed to sex of dog in CED.

- Is she still hungry afterwards?
- Does she eat?
- Is she satisfied?

The cycle protocol (Chapter Five) shows a sensory exercise or toy play in first activity puzzle piece after first relaxation. White pieces are activities, black pieces are relaxation periods.

How to make choices within cycle

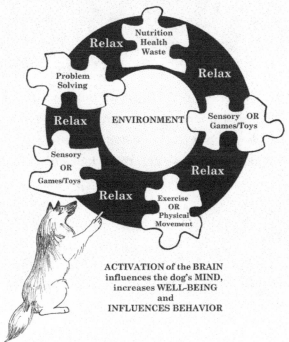

THE PATH OF THE CED
The Right Combination

Nutrition
Health
Waste

Relax

Relax

Problem
Solving

Relax

ENVIRONMENT

Sensory OR
Games/Toys

Sensory
OR
Games/Toys

Relax

Relax

Exercise
OR
Physical
Movement

ACTIVATION of the BRAIN
influences the dog's MIND,
increases WELL-BEING
and
INFLUENCES BEHAVIOR

If a dog has a hard time relaxing (hyperactive, hypokinesis, over-stimulated, over-excited, humping behaviors, over-arousal), choose a sensory exercise prior to one-hour relaxation period on the first day.

If the dog doesn't, then start with a play period and then a relaxation period. The two dogs above were different individuals that required different considerations.

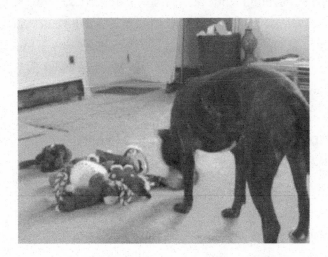

noninteractive toy play

How to for non-interactive 15-minute toy exercise

There is a non-interactive and an interactive play period in the CED both looking at different observations and patterns. Non-interactive observes if the dog can self-soothe, are they creative alone, or do they just not know what to do with the toys. The interactive toy period observes relationship between dog and pet guardian. Is pet guardian creative with play or not comfortable with it, how does the dog respond or not respond and what play activities are chosen.

How to for interactive 15-minute toy exercise: (same for interactive, except client will interact with their dog for a full 15-minutes as written below versus not interacting and just observation). Non-interactive and interactive periods are done at separate times.

First five minutes – put toys (variety) down, sit on floor and observe

Next five minutes – hide two or three toys under a cloth or blanket and go back and sit down

Last five minutes – take some treats and hide under or in some toys and pile them all up

At end of 15-minute time period look at dog and say "that'll do!" or 'all done' or any release word just so it is consistent and indicates you are done. Look away and pick up all the toys and put them away (no toy left on the floor of house anywhere and put them up high or in a toybox with a lid. It is that simple.

Questions to ask after a play period

- Is she creative?
- Does she have fun?

The role in a non-interactive play period is to put down a pile of toys and evaluate what the dog does for a full 15-minutes with no interaction. If she does nothing, then that is what will be recorded, what does she do instead? If she plays, how does she play, what does she play with, what does she do exactly?

Relaxation periods, four within one cycle

Follow activity with a relaxation period of at least one hour. Questions to ask after a period of relaxing are:

- What happens during this time?
- Can the dog relax?
- Are they calm?
- Is deep sleep achieved?
- Are they fighting sleep or faking sleep? Be specific.

Video is helpful here at timed intervals, for example at 30-minute mark, and at 45-minute mark. In order to decide what level of relaxation a dog is in, photos and video are required.

Alone time used with hyperactive types and separation anxiety

Questions to ask after an alone time observation. Alone time is for dogs who may have an over- the-top attention seeking behavior or have separation anxiety. Alone time is accomplished with the pet guardian present, but silent, often referred to as playing invisible dog. It is designed to see how the dog self–soothes or does not and what they do instead. Questions to be answered are:

- What does she do?
- How does she entertain herself?
- Does she bark?
- Pace?
- Does she settle down?
- Look for toys?
- Stick by guardian? What?

Problem-solving activities

Both dogs, in the comparison example, ended their morning with a problem-solving exercise to mentally tire. One of the three problem-solving activities was chosen, color recognition (explained in more detail in Chapter 13 – Mentally tiring games and activities).

Observation questions to ask after color recognition exercise:

- Does the dog distinguish color?
- Is the pet guardian teaching properly?
- Is she sensitive to color?
- Is the dog able to quickly understand exercise?

- Do the objects scare her?

- What egg or colored cup does she go to first?

- How does she approach the task?

- Does she think about it?

- Or move in too quickly making wrong decisions to find the food and not really looking at the color?

- Does she walk away? This could mean she is thinking.

- Does she need more encouragement? or less encouragement? Too much encouragement can confuse a dog

- Does she really enjoy participation?

Next is a continued comparison of the examples of the same two dogs after lunch, on day one. As you can see each is slightly different, yet similar because a systematic, cyclic protocol is being used.

Jersey Day One Afternoon Example – cycle to end of day one

- 1 Hour Relaxation AND warm towel

- **Interactive Toy Play**

- Body wrap – get her moving

- 1 Hour Relaxation – intent deep sleep

- Problem-solving – Size recognition

- End day with dinner, 20M digestion rest, play period outdoors, and chew to work mou**th**

Max Day One Afternoon Example

COMPLETE DAY ONE
A TALE OF TWO DOGS – Afternoon

Cycle to end of day one   **Max**

Interactive Toy Play 15M
1 Hour Relaxation – deep sleep
Wrap – get him moving
1 Hour Relaxation
Thundershirt – 15 M
Problem-solving – size recognition
1 Hour Relaxation
Dinner, 20M digestions relaxation,
     outdoor playtime, chew to work
     mouth

For the most part, both dogs had the same afternoon CED. The photos represent their bodies in day one. Max is fake relaxing and his muscles are tense. Jersey is having a hard time even lying down. The dog's body will go through noticeable changes outwardly as the muscles relax. IIt will be like looking at a different dog in most cases (as depicted in comparison photos on next pages of Jersey and Max in day three deep sleep). The process the dog usually goes through is rest, relax, calm before reaching deep sleep, non-REM to REM to non-REM. (Explained in Chapter 12 under Dear Dog Relax).

What happens internally in day one

It is important to understand the basics of what goes on inside a dog that makes for changes outwardly. Day one starts to build eustress, the feel good mood enhancing stress chemicals of oxytocin, serotonin, endorphins, and dopamine. A Companion Dog Laboratory Study shows the amount of oxytocin built correlates with how much eye contact the dog pet guardian could make with their dog. In a three day CED, the dog pet guardian will be creating a lot of eye contact and building or renewing a bond and relationship with their dog. The hormones of calm, love, relaxation, bonding, and healing are all pieces of the CED and why it works. Dogs are kept calm and an emotional bond occurs between dog and pet guardian in most cases. Many periods of relaxation are created allowing for healing to occur from the inside outwardly, the healing of emotions and stress reduction. Everything you would expect from a stress vacation.

Research studies (refer to resource references) show oxytocin reduces anxiety states, stress, addictions, and even problems of birth in breeding programs.

Day One starts to release distress, acute stress as defined by elevated levels of cortisol, adrenalin, noradrenalin or norepinephrine and neoepinephrine. When a dog is in a state of chronic versus acute stress, the levels of these chemicals are higher and the dog is in a constant state of stress. This means it may take longer than three days to achieve eustress.

Cortisol alone is naturally released in conditions of stress, infection, pain, surgery or even trauma. In excess cortisol poisons the dog's body and health issues such as Cushings Disease can occur. A low balance of cortisol can cause Addisons Disease. Cortisol in normal levels is needed to sustain life and maintain important body functions.

How to customize a day two protocol

From what is learned about the dog and the pet guardian in day one of the CED, day two is then customized to the individual. Creating a true low stress environment is a critical part. Listening and observation are also a big part of the CED and will help create the final analysis, which is the golden nugget of the process because it leads to a clear behavior modification strategy that is workable by the pet guardian and their dog.

In day one analysis occurs through client comments, video, and photos. Trouble spots will emerge and the level of relaxation the dog was able to achieve will be evident. Responsiveness level of the dog will be important in deciding what level of intensity to provide for problem-solving and other activity, as well as noting mood of pet guardian, their involvement in the process and the learning process in general.

An example of what was learned in Jersey's day one that would be not only pertinent to the final analysis, but also to customization of day two is explained below as regards the A, B, C's of antecedent (what happens prior to behavior, behavior (defined), and consequence (to the dog).

Antecedent: Jersey was sniffing a small hole in the ground.

Behavior: She gave a short growl when (male house dog) approached her hole.

Consequence: Male housedog retreated and there were no further problems. The behavior worked to deter the milder, more respectful of space male housedog.

Jersey learned resource guarding the hole in the ground worked to remove the other dog. As a result, resource guarding became a behavior to be worked on in the behavior modification process. In comments/analysis, it is important to really listen to the client and to know what you are seeing and hearing. In this case, had this not occurred and reference was made to it, resource guarding would not have been brought up and we would be missing an important piece to solving the puzzle.

At this stage it is important to ask questions and to make sure what is seen in this example is, in fact, resource guarding. Possible questions to ask at the end of day one would be, "Is there often a problem here?" Or "Is this just respected communication?" "Is your dog a resource guarder?" "Have there been other problems in this area?" It is important to know, as it means there is stress in this multi-dog household daily, not just for the dog going through the CED.

In this case the answer came back as , "yes, there were problems with resource guarding." The dog in question is a resource guarder or dog who guards resources, and has occasionally drawn blood from male dog during their arguments.

An incident had occurred three days prior to the CED. The other dog's defense was shrieking during the attack. It was also stated the two dogs were overly attached to each other most of the time.

The relevance this would have in day two is stress levels are still high and attention to environment is key to continuing the CED. There should be no contact with the other dog and no need to resource guard. Mentally tiring activity would be increased in day one to achieve calm and work toward deep sleep. The knowledge is there will be work to do between the two dogs to assure resource guarding doesn't become habituated. This would be a primary point in the resulting final analysis of the CED. The other dog is a victim, not fighting back, but doesn't trust the dog that is resource guarding. Patterns are starting to emerge.

In this case, the level relaxation was not being achieved in day one. The pet guardian confessed distractions were hard to keep down. Outside noise was distracting, such as a car door slamming causing barking. It was discovered the dog doing the CED is reactive to having her harness taken off over her head and other movement in that area. The pet guardian admitted this was probably due to a scar on the face, something that may have occurred prior to rescue.

What this indicates for the CED in day two is important, the dog's muscles were still tense and the stress from three days prior would be leading to the reason for not relaxing fully in day one. This dog was good at problem-solving and activities. Increasing not only the number of activities, but the complexity, would be particularly good for this dog. Achieving deep muscle relaxation is the goal and to note the patterns being seen to complete a solid final analysis that will serve as a behavior modification process or in addition to the functional assessment/behavior program already developed.

Returning to the example of the two dogs in day one

Here is how their morning CED continued:

In Jersey's case the color recognition was revisited due to complications in day one.

Jersey Day Two Example Morning

- BEFORE BREAKFAST – AWARENESS WALK – Exercise/ Physical Stimulation
- 20M RELAXATION to calm stomach
- BREAKFAST
- 20 M Digestion RELAXATION –
- AFTER: wrap, warm towel, walk up and back – Sensory
- GROOMING – Ttouch – Bath – Sensory
- 1 HOUR RELAXATION
- PROBLEM-SOLVING – revisted the color recognition – ADVANCED workout
- INTERACTIVE TOY PLAY
- 1 to 2 HOUR RELAXATION
- WRAP – Sensory

Jersey's Day Two Afternoon Example

- Problem-Solving – size recognition
- HEAVY ON ACTIVITY – to build that relationship back up; to mentally tire Jersey.
  - Give Take
  - Problem-solving – basket exercise
  - Obstacle course
  - Muffin Tin

- Forage for cups
- 20 M RELAXATION
- Mouthwork – CHEW
- 1 HOUR RELAXATION
- DINNER
- RELAX REST OF EVENING

Jersey's day two allowed her to ease into her day, while providing more mental activity and problem solving in the afternoon when most distractions occurred. The problem-solving activities provide an opportunity to get feedback and observation through video and photos. (See Chapter 13 – Observation and Analysis, Mentally Tiring Games and Activities)

Revelations about Max during CED

In Max's day two, a few issues had to be resolved. This gives an example of what might occur during a CED and whether the result will be to abort, redo later, or continue. Several pieces emerged during day one: Client would be unable to continue CED until early afternoon. Max would stay home with other dogs and mostly sleep. He would also go out and run around backyard.

Because then trainer, Leslie Clifton, was working behind the scenes on this case, it was chosen to customize CED further, add pieces according to the cycle, using two relaxation pieces and physical stimulation piece as backyard play for the morning.

It is important to work the cycle as it is written, in the order it is written for maximum results. Pet guardians must have valid reasons to changing the cycle. It is not recommended, but can be doable if cycle can be continued in format as written for systematic completion.

It was also revealed that Max was inseparable from one of the other dogs in house. Max likes to chew on a Nylabone and then goes back to bed in morning. He likes to be outside. The pet guardian wants Max to compete in agility and he has been balking at the start unless a squeaky toy is available. He wears a Thundershirt to Control Unleashed classes and runs away when he sees the Thundershirt come out. He enjoyed being the center of pet guardian's attention during the CED (versus two other dogs always around).

Words like inseparable set the stage for separation anxiety and in this case, reveals a close bond between two dogs in the household. This bond could help Max overcome behavior issues or could make them worse.

It also appeared Max needed to ease into his day and so the change in the morning would be helpful and not a hindrance especially if he was able to relax fully. The fact he likes to be outside was also a positive and would be used as his physical stimulation of the day, in addition to his camaraderie with the other dogs in the household. While not ideal, it would still allow him to de-stress and allow him to process the positive information from day one, and stick to the progress of the systematic nature of the CED cycle.

The Thundershirt had been poisoned because it meant Max had to go to his class and agility, which was apparent he did not want to do. It would be encouraged to make agility fun if the pet guardian wanted to continue to pursue that venue and not to put on the Thundershirt. It is as possible to condition bad associations, as it is good associations. Changing Max's association to even going to class would be a part of his behavior modification process. Since he enjoys being the center of attention this can be used to great advantage in restructuring interactions with Max. So here is what Max's day two looked like:

Max Day Two Example Morning

- Awareness Walk (loves the outdoors and observing how he handles a morning walk)
- 20M Relaxation
- Breakfast
- 20M Digestion Relaxation

- Grooming and Ttouch – Physical Stimulation
- 1 HOUR Relaxation
- Nail clipping, Bath
- Interactive Toy Play
- Problem-solving (mentally tiring) – 10 to 20 cups foraging activity
- 1 HOUR Relaxation

Max Day Two Example Afternoon

Because observation showed Max was more active in the afternoon, the activities were increased (physical stimulation + problem-solving + games/toys) to tire him.

- Obstacle Coursework – get him moving – physical stimulation
- Repeat Color Recognition
- Repeat Size Recognition
- Muffin Tin Game
- 20 M Relaxation
- CHEW to release mouth tension
- 1 HOUR Relaxation
- Interactive Toy Play
- Mock Agility Course –
- physical stimulation
- 20M Relax
- Dinner
- Relax rest of evening

Customizing day three

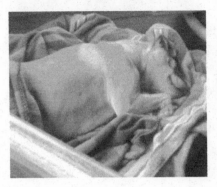

Both dogs by Day Three of the CED

Day three emphasizes sleep, day two might be more specific to mentally tiring the dog, but the cycle remains in place. In the example above, day two comments revealed further areas to pay attention to day three and in the final analysis. Patterns were formulating. The third day is further customized from what was seen in day one and day two and looked like this:

Jersey – Day Two Comments resulting in How To for Day Three

The walks are not leisurely with her whether she's alone or with another house dog. They are rapid.

- Fighting Relaxation
- Loves wraps, ttouch, warmth
- Sensitivity in hind quarters, legs
- Gets cold quickly, heat seeker
- Ran away and hid – bath.
- Jersey behavior modification concerns:
- Unsure of herself – doesn't problem solve
- Not good at "give and take"
- Loses interest

Max – Day Two Comments resulting in How To for Day Three

- Walks are enjoyable and fun. Leash stays loose. They are a team.

- Car rides are stressful.

- Loves Ttouch (esp tail work/inner thigh), Music, Warmth. Lots of sighs.

- Not good with baths or nail clipping.

- Toy play increased – exploring more

- Resource guards' toys from other dogs

- Optimal activity in afternoon/evening

- DID NOT DO mock-up agility course.

- Max behavior modification concerns:

- Doesn't feel safe, unsure

- Need to address resource guarding

- Learns quickly. Auditory keenest sense

Day three also involves evaluating waste in comparison to day one, nutrition, and health suggestions based on patterns seen so a visit to the veterinarian can be planned. This would include any pain sensitivity, movement that appeared abnormal, changes in fur, heat seeking behavior, lumps, bumps, or skin or foot issues discovered during touch exercises.

In day two carrots were added to the meal for two reasons, a sweeter taste sensation and as a carbohydrate for energy. Stress interrupts a variety of bodily functions. Stress can cause nutritional deficiencies. It can interfere with sleep and cellular regeneration.

In day three the carrots are removed and greens are added, a sour taste sensation, different texture and also energy carbohydrate as dogs move back into their original diet in the day after the CED.

The CED is a stress vacation for dogs, as well as a time of observation, understanding the dog from the inside outwardly, and finding patterns to help formulate a better and individualized behavior modification process.

The Final Analysis resulting from the CED includes an easy-to-read MSWord Smart Art (any similar program is fine) for the client and a written document explaining all the elements and steps to continue. The trainer can add to or create a functional assessment for themselves by what was learned in the 72-hour stress release process. The dog is now ready to learn better, faster and retain new information longer.

The resulting day three for Jersey and Max looked like this:

Jersey Day Three Morning Example – Goal deep sleep

- Ttouch before Breakfast
- Breakfast
- 20M digestion relaxation
- Wrap – move through obstacles
- 1 hour relaxation
- Music and Ttouch
- Relationship building
- Observation activity (Repeat 2, 3)
- 30M Relaxation (repeat 2 – dark, music)
- 1 hour relaxation

Max day Three Morning Example – Goal Deep Sleep

- Breakfast
- 20M digestion relaxation
- Problem-solving – shape acuity
- 1 hour relaxation
- Alone time (compare to day 1)
- Toys/games
- 1 hour relaxation

Jersey Day Three Afternoon Example

- Physical stimulation – outdoor
- Problem-solving – find shortest way
- 1 hour relaxation – full body wrap, dark, no distractions, music
- Problem-solving – object naming
- 1 hour relaxation – dark, music
- Chew – release mouth tension
- 1hour relaxation
- Dinner –rest – ease out of day

Max Day Three Afternoon Example

- Interactive mat game
- 1 hour Relaxation
- Physical stimulation – obstacles
- 1 hour relaxation
- Interactive toy play
- Chew – release mouth tension
- 1 hour relaxation, music
- Dinner – 20M rest – Outdoor play – chew – and/or agility coursework

Both Jersey and Max had two (versus typical one) MSWORD Smart art flow charts (examples below). Here is Jersey's resulting MSWord Smart Art: (in layers, like peeling back an onion, because Jersey is complex). The art starts with the bottom circle and moves upward in sequence.

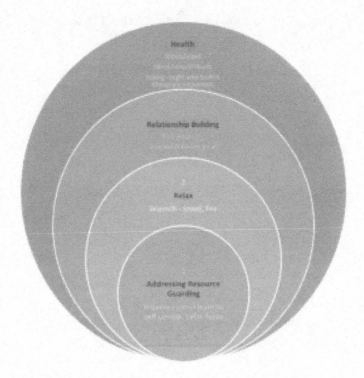

And also for Jersey, more specific to behavior modification: (start with top right, moves clockwise)

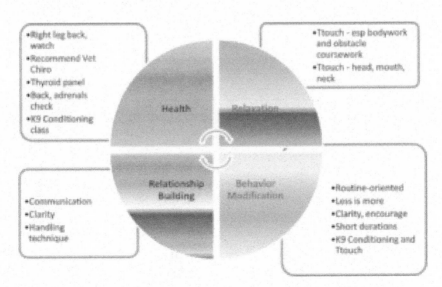

Jersey's pet guardians took the charting and CED seriously and did everything in them.

And here is Max's resulting MSWord Art for comparison: (starts at top and moves clockwise)

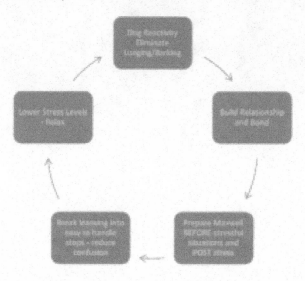

And more specific to behavior modification: (all work will extend from working with Max's dog reactivity)

Jersey and Max are unique individuals and their final analysis would not be the same. What works for one dog may not work for another.

What you need to know about dog guardians and how it affects proper implementation of the CED

Reactive dogs are like angels with one wing, they can only fly with our help. - Anonymous

Dog pet guardians want quick fixes.

About Quick Fixes

Do you know what you are seeing – or are you thinking, how am I going to "fix" this or "get rid" of this behavior. If a dog has a hair trigger reaction – do you know what is happening internally? How would knowing that the dog is not sleeping well, gulping its food have on the way you would work with this dog? How does knowing help us as trainers? Quick fixes could take up a whole chapter alone. See my blog on this topic in resource section.

Since this is a book focusing on force free techniques and results, quick fixes have typically been thought of as a wording choice of aversive or traditional trainer and considered successful only in short-term. If you have a problem with your dog, identify the cause. Long-term dog training solutions are better than quick fixes and provide lasting results. If quick fixes worked, there would be no need for dog trainers, or psychiatrists and psychologists for that matter. The reality is you need to address the behavior. It's the old saying, " give a man a fish and you feed him for a day; teach a man to fish and you feed him for a lifetime." It is the same with behavior modification. It is best to address the dog's behavior long-term and that starts with conscientious stress release and maintaining normal stress levels throughout the dog's behavior modification. Pet guardians do not look at nor understand their dogs like a professional. The reality is guardians:

- don't know that stress affects canines too
- may not know their dog has health issues that can affect behavior and be caused by stress
- may be on their last straw, their last nerve, and don't understand that the more a dog repeats a behavior, the more they will
- don't have a plan or a clue how to work with their dog and need help
- are busy and want the dog to fit, rather than teach the dog how to fit
- adopt dogs with issues
- think dogs come to them pre-trained
- may not understand their dog's body language
- have stress in their everyday life that affect the dog too
- are often confused about how to train 'teach' their dog, what method to use
- compare a beloved past dog with the one they have now

The trainer should plan to focus intensely on the CED on a case by case basis. Doing one at a time, along with a normal workload is recommended. It is more intense than doing a private session. Trainer will send guardian a "customized" step-by-step day and the explanations behind each step (use sample in Chapter 11 or see examples in appendix).

In review, dog guardians receive guidelines and will be required to take digitals and/or video of the CED in progress for reference, review, and observation. Each case should have a signed permission form allowing use of photographs, video, and comments. (Sample Appendix 3). As a matter of policy, a CED should also have a specific liability form should be signed by participant. (Sample Appendix 4).

At the end of each day of the CED in progress, the pet guardian will need to answer several questions. Day's two and three are customized to the individual canine and developed based on what is seen in day one. Day one is customized as to behavior. (Sample in appendix 5) Additions or deletions to day one are explained in follow-up note in Appendix 2.

The CED should end each day by 6:00 p.m. and ease into a relaxing evening with family and then into a continuous eight hours of sleep. Undisturbed sleep is the goal at night. Six p.m. is a good time to shoot for to have the guardian complete the day's comments, and to send digitals and video, but any time toward early to late evening is acceptable according to their schedule. The pet guardian can also opt to send comments and observations as they go through the process. The trainer must have time to compile the next day's schedule and the pet guardian must have time to review it to get off to a good start. The start of each day sets the tone for the entire day and resulting activities. The templates will help the process go faster.

The goal of the CED is to achieve deep REM sleep. This is where stress starts to release, to renew, to energize. To do so is a process. The process is systematic rest, relaxation, calming and then deep sleep. What does it look like and how is it accomplished?

Chapter 12

Sleep Stages

Photos showing the difference between body tone within three days (side by side) Photo 1: Bo day one, tension throughout body; Photo 2: Bo day three, tension released

- A successful canine emotional detox stress release protocol will release or neutralize bad stress and build good stress (eustress)

- change the way a dog feels internally and looks physically, releasing muscle tension

- change the way a dog feels emotionally

- provide deep non-REM and (REM), heavy sleep

- complete several problem-solving activities to mentally tire

- reveal how the dog handles real life through identified patterns seen during course of three days

- renew dog and pet guardian relationship and bond

The three elements of a final analysis are the CED's golden nuggets:

- Client, foster, trainer comments are golden, as are video, digital reviews

- Discovering patterns within the CED can save a dog's life

- Final analysis pulls the CED together and can formulate the resulting behavior modification process and skills program individualized to the dog and guardian

Dear Dog, Relax – The Process and what it looks like

Photo to left Doobie under blanket Photo right, Buddy resting on dog bed

To left is Doobie in beginning stages of relaxation using a warm towel to relax muscle tension. To right is Buddy in mid-stages of relaxation, still showing muscle tension but head and neck becoming heavy. Buddy has a warm, cozy bed to set the stage for deep sleep. Warmth has a sensory element and a calming effect to help induce sleep and release muscle tension.

The process the dog goes through in the CED to attain deep sleep is rest, relax (fake, fighting sleep can occur in these two stages), calm (but easily distracted), deep sleep, non-REM to REM to non-REM (not distracted). It is a process. It cannot be forced. It must happen willingly and systematically. Deep sleep is where healing starts and is important in starting to change the behavior of challenging dogs. The guardian sets the stage, but does not ask the dog to lie down.

Achieving deep sleep

Questions to ask are: Does dog sleep so soundly that when there is movement, such as guardian moving around or away, that they do not get up, follow, or watch? This is the goal to achieve in the CED.

Does dog get a quality 12 to 14-hours of sleep per day, eight at night, undisturbed, and two to four during the day? Is the stage set for dog to achieve daytime relaxation periods?

Why ask these questions? Why are these questions important? Dogs need to deeply sleep to keep stress at normal levels and that is the bottom line. It is as important as exercise and mental problem-solving. It allows the body to heal and to release stressful chemicals bottled up in the body and brain. It allows the body to build eustress, the good stress, for mood-enhancing and energy replacement. Deep sleep releases tight muscle tension throughout the body and allows the dog to process positive information better.

The CED's main goal is deep relaxation, non-REM followed by REM sleep, inspired by mentally tiring activity, toy play, positive sensory input, physical stimulation and setting the scene (the environment) to accomplish deep sleep.

As you see in the CED cycle/pathway, there are five relaxation pieces in one cycle rotation. The first and last relaxation periods in the cycle are a 20-minutes post-eating rest to aid in digestion. The other relaxation periods are at least 60-minutes with a goal toward processing the good information that occurred before that relaxation period and to try and achieve deep sleep for building serotonin reserves and melatonin in non-REM sleep.

Sleep is the result of an integrated action of the central nervous system. During sleep and wakefulness there are many different and even apparently opposite changes. Dog sleep behavior is evaluated based on the age, breed and personality of the dog. A puppy up to five months will need more sleep, an adolescent less, and adult dogs based on breed and personality. Too much or too little sleep can indicate health problems. The dog guardian will become more aware of their dogs sleep habits and be able to understand and detect problems before they get out of hand.

It sounds easier than it is to achieve. A dog who is chronically or acutely stressed will have a very hard time achieving deep sleep. Deep sleep is only accomplished in a step-by-step systematic way and should calm the dog's brain and release muscle tension throughout the body. In deep sleep, a dog will wake up at first looking like they don't know where they are, they might lie back down and distractions will be irrelevant. The dog will be less tense in appearance. The dog is ready to learn without all the baggage and distress.

Once a dog doesn't feel stressed, noticeable changes start to occur and a behavior modification and skill's application process becomes more successful to implement.

Here is the process of achieving deep sleep as created for the CED. These steps are what has been seen in over 700 completed CED cases.

Analyzing sleep stages Rest to Relax to Calm leads to non-REM to REM and back out to non-REM

A dog's sleep patterns are like human sleep patterns. There are three stages of sleep. The first phase is non-rapid eye movement (NREM). In addition, there are three stages of NREM, phases N1, N2, and N3. N1 is the first stage of NREM and is a transition to unconsciousness; the dog loses control over his muscles but you may notice some movement in the limbs.

N2 is a stage characterized by sleep spindles; there is some brain activity involved, but the dog is very calm during the N2 stage. N2 is the lengthiest sleep stage, lasting for up to 45% of the total sleeping time.

N3 is also known as the slow wave stage. During the slow wave the dog has a decreased heart rate, lower blood pressure, decreased body temperature and breathes slowly. During this phase, the dog sleeps deeply and he does not react to noises or other disruptions even if they are loud.

The slow wave phase lasts for 10 to 15 minutes and is followed by the rapid eye movement phase (REM). This is an active phase and the dog seems more agitated during the sleep. You may notice his eyes rolling and the dog may even whine or bark and move his limbs. There is brain activity during the REM phase and there are certain theories according to which dogs have dreams. The REM phase lasts for 10 to 15% of the total sleeping time. Puppies will spend more time in the REM phase.

As a trainer doing CEDs and analyzing where a dog is in relation to sleep determines where they are in the stress cycle. It is important to evaluate and know what is seen, so it can be determined if a dog is simply distressed, acutely stressed or chronically stressed. This knowledge will affect how to proceed with this dog in a behavior modification format.

There are steps leading up to deep sleep.

Bo in resting posture

Rest. First resting will occur meaning ears (alert to sound), eyes (open), mind is still very active and the dog is possibly lying on stomach with back legs poised to move, or with hips to one side, and might even put head on paws with eyes wide open, ears taking in all sounds, like radar.

Relax. Relax will follow as dog moves to side of hip, head down, no radar, eyes closed, but mind is still active. Dog is feeling safe and so muscles are starting to relax a bit. A dog can fake relaxing or fight relaxing and can pop up as soon as someone moves or they hear a sound. The goal is always that the dog can deeply sleep and not worry about distractions, or someone getting up and moving.

The next three steps lead to deep sleep. In a chronically stressed dog (where a dog cannot come down below threshold), the process will take longer than three days. A distressed (short spikes of stress) and an acutely stressed individual (high spikes that go over threshold) means the dog does go over threshold, but can come back down within eight to 72-hours. This is average for most dogs. CED findings show 10% of dogs are chronically stressed.

Calm. The third stage is complete calm. At this stage the pet guardian will start to hear the dog sigh, yawn, eyes will blink, neck will start to appear too heavy to hold up and dog may melt further into relaxing or lie on their side completely. If you start to see some of these signs in first and second days, it means the dog is only distressed or acutely stressed and a 72-hour stress release process will be all that is needed. However, only working through the entire three days can this be confirmed.

Annie in non-REM

Then the beginnings of sleep start to occur, the stages of NREM, as described earlier. The body is visibly less tense, and head and shoulders are heavy. Ears are softer, wrinkle in forehead disappears, jowls become loose.

Zoe a puddle of fur

To achieve deep sleep non-REM to REM and back to non-REM must occur within the body. This is where the body heals itself and is a complex process. What it looks like is what I call a puddle of fur, as seen in the photo of Zoe above. The dog deeply sleeps, aware of nothing, body is totally melted and tense free, muscles soft. The dog will noticeably look different. When people move or distractions occur the dog does not get up or move, and when they finally wake up they look floppy, disheveled, not fully awake yet and might not know where they are in that moment. They might flop back down and continue sleeping. Basically, it takes time coming out of REM (rapid eye movement) to non-REM and to fully awaken. This is when stress releases. It feels good, the dog wants to repeat it. Deeper sleep starts to become easier.

Relaxation and stress release accelerators

Set the stage. Setting the stage, creating a safe environment is key to stress release. Here are a few ways to do this.

Create a safe zone. A safe zone is a low distraction, cozy place dog will associate with sleeping (a crate, a room, a mat, a corner of room with cozy dog bed).

Music. Play indoors at timed periods and/or outdoors at timed periods with goal that dogs lie down indoors/outdoors and rests. Music becomes the predicting cue to sleep. Outdoors provide elevated platforms and cozy areas.

Tellington Touch (Ttouch) Wraps or a Thundershirt. A wrap or Thundershirt (www.thundershirt.com) allows body to relax, and should represent relaxation NOT activity. Wraps can also be used to help with mindful movement of an animal. This movement can help the brain focus on alignment of the body and can also provide a relaxing experience. Read more about wraps for animals and humans at www.tellingtontouch.com.

Warm towel or blanket. Most dogs respond well to warmth, some prefer cold so comfort, coziness needs to be redefined for those dogs with the goal always to relax muscles and release tension. Simply toss a towel or blanket, a Thundershirt or t-shirt into a dryer and take out as it is tumbling to retain warmth. Then place on body and record dogs response.

Relaxing, soft tone of voice. Read to dog, softly talk to them, do some slow, soothing petting or Ttouch, and/or do calming signals (yawn, deep breath, lip lick, turn head away). Audio books on low are a good way to provide a relaxing atmosphere.

The importance of sleep for dogs

The body fights for homeostasis constantly. Non-REM and REM sleep are both important for physiological and psychological health. In dogs, sleep state is measured by behavioral and EEG criteria.

Definition of NREM and REM sleep

Non-REM , non-rapid eye movement (NREM). During non-REM (NREM) breathing is slower, deeper, and less variable than during wakefulness.

REM, rapid eye movement (REM). REM is characterized by rapid, shallow, and irregular breathing. Sleep, deep sleep, is important to the dog for mental acuity, functioning normally, learning, behavioral soundness and processing information, and health.

How calm is different from deep relaxation

Wakefulness versus deep sleep is the difference. Maintaining calm in the face of distractions or real life occurrences can be taught, but it does not involve deep sleep or a state of deep relaxation. For the CED, achievement of deep NREM, REM sleep is the goal. To get to that goal various levels of relaxation occur.

In case after case it was observed that in day two behavior might get worse before it gets better. As stress chemicals start to release the dog feels differently (many dogs don't know what it is like to not be stressed) and is like coming down from an induced chemical high (drugs or alcohol). Relaxation to calm to deep sleep is always key to the healing process, to neutralize stress chemicals and build good stress (mood enhancers, love hormones, feel good hormones). (Go to "How To" section, Chapter 11 and "Chapter Three -How to tell if a dog is stressed and its severity")

Chapter 13

Observation and Analysis of Mentally Tiring Games and Activities

"Dogs, just like people, have different talents. Some dogs find it hard to impossible to figure out a task, while others can solve it in no time. But even dogs that are "learning resistant" are perfectly loveable and need your affection. Give them simpler tests and exercises to do. Take your pet's personality into account." - Immanuel Birmelin, Biologist

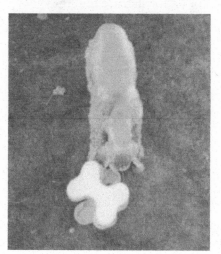 

Photo 1 – Charlie intelligence puzzle, the Tornado Photo 2 – Henry has trouble with toy play

Charlie, to left, enjoys a purchased intelligence game called a Tornado, a Nina Ottosson puzzle, while Henry, to right, has difficulty figuring out how to creatively play by himself with selected toys. The favorite part of most dog pet guardians and trainers is the problem-solving activities and mentally tiring games to include toy play. As humans, we tend to gravitate toward what is fun.

Take a look at the CED cycle (Chapter Six, The Right Combination) and the second puzzle piece indicates to choose a sensory OR game/toy activity. How to decide which one is to pay attention to the individual. If a dog has digestive issues, or is very hyperactive or barks a lot choose a sensory activity first (especially on Day One), because the way we start the day makes a difference in the rest of the day and how the dog progresses. The first exercise would then include a warm towel or blanket from the dryer (or lying in the sun undisturbed). Sensory focuses on sight, hearing, touch, taste, scent. Any one of these can comprise a sensory application.

Dogs who love to play, who love toys or who are performance dogs who like to be active choose a game session of 15-minutes (your choice is non-interactive or interactive toy play) or an intelligence toy. These dogs usually must have a lot of activity to mentally tire. If that is the case, for instance in day two using observation of dog's play and if a pattern is seen, then add more consecutive games activities, up to three in a row, before next relaxation period. Add pieces in any area, but do not delete them.

"When dogs become useful, we develop an affection for them." Clive Wynne

What the CED goes for with these selected exercises is to tire the brain and body, which achieves deep REM sleep (discussed in Chapter 12).

What does the activities portion of the CED accomplish?

The activities help build a better relationship between dog and pet guardian. The activities reveal how a dog processes what they are learning. Activities create a base to where a dog is in the learning continuum. All this helps proceed with a customized behavior modification program to help the dog be successful, while building eustress, the good stress chemicals that enhance the learning experience, create confidence and give renewed energy and well-being.

Relationship building

Relationship building is important, especially if a dog guardian has lost trust in their dog. From mentally stimulating activities, interactive play, energy releasing activity, working on key pieces of behavior modification and scheduled full rest periods, guardian and dog will not only come to see each other in a new light, but will build positive associations while the bad stress chemicals release from the body so learning replaces confusion and inconsistency. The whole family can be involved in this critical stress releasing period.

What do the activities reveal about the dog?

The unreliable canine. The definition of unreliable is one of not being dependable or untrustworthy. Activities will reveal this in many ways. Is the dog eager to do the task or do they walk away, give up, don't even try? Does the pet guardian find themselves becoming frustrated because the dog doesn't or isn't able to carry out a simple task? Does the dog growl at, back away, refuse to participate? This is a dog who is unreliable, one who needs to gain trust and feel safe before they can even start an in-depth behavior modification or skills program. Patience, perseverance and a specific plan is needed to progressively work with and move this dog forward.

As you can see already the mentally tiring activities are formulated to observe how the dog processes information, learns, participates. The activities evaluate how stressed the dog has become. Let's look at what else the activities will reveal.

The short sessions are better canine. This is the dog that 10 to 20 repetitions will stress them out, not release stress. This dog may very well just need one or two repetitions in the beginning with the objective to increase duration slowly and incrementally. This is the way the behavior modification process will need to go for this dog, meaning short sessions, keeping sessions successful and a lot of rest periods in between training.

The irritable canine. Usually health issues are the reason for the irritable canine. This dog will have a lot of stress signals from licking themselves, itching, scratching, shaking it off, yawning, rapid tongue flicks and more to avoid an activity or during an activity or even after the activity is over. This is usually the dog who doesn't like to be touched, will snap if certain parts of body are touched, and who just a simple activity becomes too much for them.

Dogs might be dealing with a combination of the above and the games might reveal other positive attributes as well, such as a dog who likes to burrow, or chew, or likes certain types of toys or activity. These can be used as functional rewards during behavior modification or as a clue to what this dog needs to be doing in their life to be building eustress. This section will reveal the eager-to-please dog, the dog who doesn't want to stop learning, the dog who tires easily, and so much more. It is a time to observe what the dog does, how they process information and not a time to institute an obedience program.

Observation and analysis

While the CED is to release distress, chronic/acute stress through deep sleep, getting there reveals much about the individual. During the entire process, especially mentally tiring activities and games, trainers (dog guardians) will want to write down and observe, making answers detailed and specific:

- How does the dog play?

- How does the dog relax? How long does it take?

- What is dog's problem-solving style?

- Does dog have the ability to focus? Does dog lose focus?

- Does dog enjoy food? Are there any problems while dog is eating?

- Does the dog have the ability to withstand boring stuff or repetition? Can dog concentrate on task?

- Does the dog enjoy husbandry interactions, such as grooming and touch?

Let's look at the problem-solving details. There are five problem-solving activities likely to be a part of a CED. How Dogs Think by Biologist Immanuel Birmelin is the source for the specific problem-solving activities in the CED. Birmelin's book has an end chapter on daily mental activities that is a valuable resource to use postCED.

These five are chosen to take a look at sensory, to evaluate how a dog thinks that could be beneficial in a results-oriented behavior modification process, and to further evaluate stress levels and triggers. Color recognition can evaluate whether the dog has a keen eyesight or not and used as an eye test, while size and shape problems evaluate if a dog is a systematic thinker, or just does what worked the first time. Do they use their nose only, or do they think, or do they do nothing, or do they have a fear of objects? The clue test is a more advanced problem and evaluates how guardian handles teaching their dog, as well as how observant dog is in interacting with guardian.

Color Recognition

- **Set-up:** Three to six different colored cups, bowls, or Easter egg halves. One should be yellow or blue.

- **Beginner level**: Yellow or blue will be the color the reward is under OR

- **Advanced level** dogs: a click/treat is given for offering a nose touch to the correct color.

NOTE: Most dogs will not be at the beginner level. Some dogs will be highly fearful of objects or even learning and will be at **remedial learning level**, revising to just one cup, with treat on top of cup or cup on side and treat close by, or cup lip resting on a reward making it highly successful for these dogs. NOT being able to do this exercise at all, even at most remedial level, simply means you need to build this dog's confidence slowly, by introducing objects and making learning fun.

Each dog will have their own style of learning and interaction.

Process: (Beginner level; revise to Advanced Level (touch/click/reward)

Do 10 to 20 repetitions with just yellow to commit the color to memory.

Then add a second container, different color.

The reward will always be under the yellow container (or blue, if chosen), no matter how many containers or in what location. These are the colors dogs can see most vibrantly.

Then add a third, a fourth etc. doing 10 to 20 repetitions each time and writing out observations. Most dog will only be able to do two, three will be challenging and raise frustration and another level of distraction.

Some dogs may be able to do up to six.

You want to see at least an 80% success rate before moving to the next color addition. This means that if you do 10 repetitions that eight out of the 10 are 100% successful. If this is not reached, continue with current exercise until it is achieved.

From this exercise, the information you gain for a progressive behavior modification process will be:

1. Can dog handle the objects, the exercise? If not, can they handle the remedial version? If so, then you will need to start behavior modification with helping the dog to relax, gain focus and build confidence before any behavior modification process starts.

2. Does dog move too quickly? OR does dog need to think and study? All of this will help you design a customized behavior modification process. Moves quickly means help dog to focus, to concentrate and also means guardian will need to think quickly and meet dogs thought process. Slow and needs to think and study, means not to rush dog through behavior modification, let them think, process and build confidence while highly rewarding success.

3. A dog who does nothing, simply means revisions and starting from the beginning in any learning. A second CED may be required, after one month OR a continuous consecutive day CED of more than three days. This dog is usually so stressed learning is awfully hard and will take patience from guardian.

Size Recognition
(like color recognition, but dealing with size)

Annie

Set-up:
- Containers neutral color (no yellow, no blue) and start with two. SUGGESION: use the small size first. It would be okay to use a large container versus a small container, but be consistent. Then use the dramatically larger one, or dramatically smaller one when a second container is added.

- (Do a few warm-ups with one – the small container – about 10 to 20).

- Then add a second container, the largest size. The largest (or the smallest) will help dog be successful, as the will be easily identified. The reward will always be under the small container (or large), no matter how many (at this stage) containers or in what location it ends up. *See above notes in color recognition for*

Remedial, Beginner, and Advanced set-ups.
- THEN add a third size. Usually a size in between small and large.
- Do 10 to 20 repetitions each. Write out observations.

- You want to see at least an 80% success rate before moving to the next size.

The Clue Test
TESTING: How well the dog understands clues.

Set-up:
- Place two stools or small tables next to each other. Put an inverted cup on each one.

- Dog should be on a sit/stay about 3 feet in front of these items. Guardian is behind the items.

- Hide a reward under ONE of the cups while dog watches.

- On TOP of the cup place an object (a tennis ball or favorite toy from toy play in Day One).

- Then hide the two stools behind a sheet or blanket.

- Switch the cups. The location of the reward

- Put the tennis ball on top of the cup that contains the reward.

Performance:

Now remove the sheet and ask dog to find it. If they go for the right cup, tilt the cup over and give a treat. If they made the wrong decision, they get nothing. REPEAT 3X. OR until dog realizes the cup containing the object has the reward. Some dogs take up to 10 repetitions to come to that understanding. Some will fail the test completely – that is okay – watch for signs of stress. Evaluate how the dog performed the exercise.

Object Recognition

Objective: Can dog recognize differences between two or more objects by name

This is a naming exercise. For the CED it looks at how attentive the dog is and their learning style. Do they have to take time to think about it? OR are they quick to go to item names? OR do they lose focus and make mistakes?

Set up:

- Choose three items. One should be familiar to dog, such as their ball. Other two should be unfamiliar. These will be named and taught during the exercise.

- Present familiar item first

- Place item in front of you. Dog should be sitting about 3 to 5 feet away on a stay.

- Say, "Find BALL" (or whatever familiar object you are using and are already confident dog knows name of it)

- Repeat 3 to 5 times. Ten remove ball behind back, in a box, or simply hide from view.

- Teach the name of next item.

- Repeat 10 to 20 times until you are certain dog has learned the name of this object.

- Remove object. Wait a few seconds to a minute.

- Bring out familiar object and newly taught object.

- Place them in front of you with dog sitting 3 to 5 feet away and on a stay.

- Objects should be about two to three feet apart.

- Start with familiar object, say, "Find BALL".

- Wait, let dog think. How do they think? Observe.

- Mark and reward a successful result.

- Then reposition and use strange object newly learned. Say "Find (OBJECT NAME) Wait. Let dog think. What do they do? If they get it wrong, it simply means more time with second object needs to be spent, so go back to naming just that object and then pair again with familiar object.

- REPEAT this process with third object. Teaching name first. Then adding it with familiar item, then to second learned item. If dog is successful, then and only then add all three. What happens?

Shape Recognition

Objective: Recognizing symbols and to test dog's power of observation

Charlie

Set-up:

- Gather three identical food bowls that are same size, color and shape.
- Cut three squares out of white cardboard.
- Draw a circle on one square with black marker. You can color them in if you wish.
- Draw a triangle on one.
- Draw a square on one.
- Place the reward (food) in the bowl that will be covered by the triangle drawn on the white cardboard. This symbol will ONLY contain food.

Performance:

- Give "find it" cue using just bowl with triangle. Repeat 10 to 20 times or more so dog can commit symbol to memory before adding a second bowl and symbol.
- Add second bowl and place cardboard piece with circle on top over the bowl. No food is in this bowl. The dog learns to identify the triangle as the only symbol that contains food in the bowl.

The dog might make an error and choose the bowl with the circle, but will quickly learn that there is no food.

- When dog has an 80% success rate going to bowl with triangle no matter location, then add third bowl with a square placed on top. Again no food is ever in this bowl.

How does the dog respond? Do they hesitate? Do they go right to the triangle? Do they test the square? What do they do when you switch the locations around?

This exercise can be advanced by adding other symbols and bowls, such as a hexagon, an octagon, and a polygon.

Does dog look to you for help? Do they get confused? Do they lie down? Do they show stress signals such as scratching or licking themselves? Do they avoid the task altogether? If so, end immediately and go back to two bowls and end on success. Much like trigger stacking in the environment, a dog can get uneasy, confused, stressed and become reactive as triggers appear and make focusing more difficult.

Using observation and analysis to go beyond the CED Ten ways to use problem-solving games in behavior modification

Mental, intelligence games and problem-solving activities can be used in a behavior modification.

Program to get results in behavior change. Games are used in environmental enrichment, but why couldn't they be used in behavior modification? How would that look?

Let's explore the 10 ways purchased enrichment, DIY enrichment and problem-solving activities can be used to modify and change behavior. These can be implemented postCED to keep on track. Thinking is mentally tiring and satisfying for a dog. Once observations are gathered on how an individual thinks, then a customized behavior modification process can begin and include some of the combination choices below. Expanding findings in a CED can help with changing behavior.

1 Human reactive dogs.

As a part of a step-by-step counter conditioning and desensitization (CC&DS) process in changing how a dog approaches a human, games can also be used to make humans appear less worrisome. Distance and duration are, of course, key with incremental increases and decreases, using first trainer, then family members, then strangers.

In using games to change behavior, a foraging game or intelligence game can be set up between the person and dog. Dog is, at first, on leash at first and has been pre-acclimated to games. The dog should enjoy interacting with games and with their guardian.

A form of counter conditioning, which means pairing something the dog likes with something the dog is anxious about or reacts to, a game can be used this way: dog approaches the game, interacts with the game while human is present at a predetermined distance and dog is approaching human without reaction, going toward game, and being rewarded throughout the game. The game focuses the dog, the strange human presence is nonthreatening and nonconfrontational, dog's mind is on the task and enjoyment of the game and rewards.

2 Fence chasing and over-barking behavior.

Providing an environmental enrichment course makes an outdoor area take on new meaning and keeps a dog's mind busy. First reduce yard access to fence with xpens (exercise pens) or an inner yard made up of x-pens where the dog goes first with goal to slowly expand area. See photo of Charlie in this chapter working on a puzzle in the yard as the mailman delivers mail.

Set up an outdoor enrichment area, which includes identifying what the dog loves to do. In one case rocks were of higher value than food.

Finding what a dog loves is key and reinforcing behavior wanted. Is it food, toys, tennisballs or something else.

Hide that item under cups or containers throughout the outdoor enrichment area. Release the dog to find and then use to desensitize and counter condition to distractions (real life or mock ups). These distractions could be a person walking by, a fake dog set up across street, a real dog and person walking by, timing to mail truck or mailman's arrival . Add variety daily, such as intelligence games, bowl exercises and expand enrichment as the yard slowly expands in area. Changing the habit of the dog in yard is the goal. What do you want the dog to do instead? This could be teaching only alert barking, a quiet look and showing no interest in fence chasing because enrichment keeps the dog busy and satisfied.

3 Dog stressed in class

Take out a game and allow dog to work on it behind a barrier or in classroom.

A stressful situation becomes something to look forward to. Great for reactive dog classes or confidence building classes. Dogs working on puzzles are not focused on other dogs or people in the room. They begin to realize they can be in the presence of other dogs safely, as well as people.

4 Resource Guarding and Counter Surfing

Providing multiple games as feeding receptacles can take the focus away from a bowl guarder. Teaching a dog the off cue by using a foraging toy makes new habits for location guarding. Off becomes fun. This can also be used to stop counter surfing.

5 Isolation and Separation anxiety.

Games are very helpful in setting up an indoor find it course. This should occur slowly and incrementally for dog anxious about their people leaving them alone. Setting up a find it course first when guardian is in same room, then leaves periodically, then sets up course and leaves immediately and so on. Leaving equals that good things flow when guardian leaves. Soon the dog will be happy to see their guardian go.

The key here is to know your dog, what is it that they love versus what you think they love. Having something to do changes the habit of the seeing you grab the keys, head out the door, and expect the dog to exist with nothing to work their mind (like closing you in a room with no books, crafts, tools etc.). Variety is the key. In the beginning short duration, working up to longer times away. The anxiety of their person leaving starts to equal fun begins. This works when the dog finds games to be of value to them and enjoy working on them.

6 Confidence building.

Starting with the easiest of easy puzzles or homemade games, like a muffin tin filled with balls and food under the balls or a braid filled with treats. A dog's confidence can improve and for fearful dogs that is key to thriving not just surviving. Some dogs are not able to do puzzles at first or even foraging games. So breaking down the games into very tiny pieces to accomplish successfully incrementally builds the dog's confidence to try ever harder problem solving.

7 Show/performance dogs.

A great relaxer and focus pre-show and post-show de-stressor. If a dog is worried about the other dogs or the crowd or noises, the games really help redirect focus onto other visuals. Can take mind off and curb performance anxiety. It can be a great tension reliver post-performance.

8 Point to point training for fearful dogs.

Set up a mat and a game or two to look forward to and then walk slowly to the point and incrementally increase the distance the mat and toy are from point A, the doorway. Works with dogs stressed with real life, neighborhood sounds etc. Each point is measured out and the dog now has a purpose other than fearing the environment or reacting to it.

9 To teach a dog how to play and to enjoy playing

Many dogs do not know how to play or were discouraged from playing. The dog may have become afraid to play and so this takes the edge off. A regular, several minutes long play time with a start cue and an end cue can make playtime something to look forward to no matter where the dog is in that learning curve. At first, the dog might not play at all. But with time and variety, toy play becomes something to look forward to and enjoy. It is a great laboratory for real life learning.

10 Relationship building

Games like cup shuffling or food find games, putting a reward on a strip of cloth and covering it with a non-moveable cover (dog must pull out reward by studying and discovering the reward is on the cloth); color recognition; size recognition and more help build relationships that have eroded and can be used in a progressive behavior modification process.

Chapter 14

How a dog plays

"PLAY is built into the nervous system as an urge. Playful behavior reflects joyful feelings. Bringing playfulness back into the therapeutic environment, intentionally and with finesse, can have profound therapeutic effects." - Jaak Panksepp

A canine emotional detox (CED) involves play activities. This is especially critical when you have a situation where the pet guardian says "My dog doesn't know how to play." OR "My dog doesn't like to play."

These statements are a clue and a cue that this dog needs to learn to play because they do not have emotional outlets. Energy release, the ability to solve problems successfully, ability to interact with pet guardians positively, and creative thinking create a state of learning where the dog can see themselves operating in the environment in a successful, positive way without incident.

Play as Stress Reduction

In one recorded case after another, the research has shown that play has a huge roll in behavior change. How a dog plays can also signify how they handle real life. That is what the CED is all about, releasing stress so behavior changes to make behavior modification programs more effective.

It entails understanding the dog on many levels, as well as the pet guardian. Bring these two elements together and change is imminent. Play releases stress, play is mentally stimulating, as well as tiring, and builds relationships and bonds.

Play styles vary from observations indicating social deficits and lack of learning to play, to eager and creative play styles. Think of play as a dog's laboratory helping them learn about real life and to exercise their natural instincts.

Taking a look at how the dog plays when no one is interacting with them versus when someone interacts is a piece of the CED that reveals if the dog can creatively interact on their own with toys, do they have favorite toys, do they play or don't they play, and simply what exactly do they do?

The interactive toy play with the pet guardian looks at the dog's relationship with their person, how does the client motivate their dog? Do they get frustrated or tired or do they enjoy playing with their dog or not? Does the dog enjoy playing with their human, do they initiate play, run away, lie down, or do not participate at all? What is seen during these periods of toy play. How the dog plays tells a lot about how they are spending their time.

Pogo and toy play Pogo, mini-poodle, is partially blind in this photo but he loves to play with toys, especially if there are hidden food rewards.

Let's look at what was learned from the way one pet guardian played with her dog and how the CED helped in analysis.

Bonnie, female Black Lab

The main issues with Bonnie were separation anxiety, dog reactivity (particularly with high energy/ arousal dogs), and resource guarding. Her pet guardian, R. Clarkson, Australia said:

"She is very quick to reach threshold, and it is getting hard to train due to this and her huge amount of triggers. In short her anxiety is preventing any real progress with her separation anxiety training. She is so used to being stressed, I don't think she has ever experienced total calm."

Here are the first five minutes Bonnie played with no interaction from Clarkson. What was observed?

A pile of toys is just set out nearby. The session is 15-minutes long.

- at first she shows no interest
- starts chewing one of the soft toys (cat)
- started chewing a plastic bottle
- distracted by a noise and leaves room
- comes back in with stolen bread from counter

Bread was more self-rewarding for Bonnie than the toys. She is a food hound. While it is important to training, it is also a reason to prevent and manage resource guarding. Same with the observation that she "kept returning to kitchen" to see if there was something easier to get food from. Bonnie is an active forager, scrounger and loses focus because it is a primary reinforcer for her.

What does this say about Bonnie? She is an "easy way is always better" type of dog. Why work if she can self-reward easily? Suggestion to Clarkson was to make sure Bonnie doesn't get self-rewarded from things left out in kitchen. This also encourages resource guarding. Suggested solution was to get lots of food type toys, whether bought or homemade, to keep Bonnie's seeking system working, one of the emotional systems as defined by Jaak Panksepp, PhD. She has a strong seeking system and needs to use it. If she isn't using it productively, she will use it her way.

Each piece in the CED stress protocol has a reason and observational value. Learning more about the individual and how they think has definite value in creating a results-oriented behavior modification program. What was observed in Bonnie's second five-minutes of non- interactive toy play, where toys are covered by a blanket?

- She lays on the blanket
- She sniffs at and digs into blanket
- She is uninterested
- She walked away
- She laid down directly in front of blanket
- She kept returning to the kitchen table (where the chicken for next part of toy play was)

What occurred in the final five-minutes of toy play, where food was hidden in and around the toys? By what was observed so far, it is evident what will occur.

- interested right away
- dug and sniffed at blanket on top of the toys
- found the toys with food first, did not interact with others at all
- once food was gone, she stopped interacting with them and lost interest

Although interest focused on the food, later just seeing the toys paired with the food will generate interest in toy play. The association to the toys will become stronger with or without food. The pet guardian was asked questions about the toy play exercise.

Is she creative?

Clarkson said, *"When there is food motivation involved, she holds the toy in her paws and sniffs it out. She tried chewing different parts of toy to get food (plastic and plush). She shook and tossed the toys too."*

This is where Bonnie starts functioning cognitively. What does that mean? Cognition is the mind flexibly solving problems. It allows for inferential reasoning (allowing for mental trial and error or this worked, that worked, this did not) leading to flexible problem-solving and relies on observable, internal mental processes. Figuring out how to get the food various ways is problem-solving. If Bonnie is faced with a problem involving food (as in more advanced exercises such as, size recognition, color recognition, or basket game) she will start to think.

Does she have fun? Clarkson said, *"Her body was relaxed, but not sure."*

The joy that a dog has when playing is hard to miss. Not being sure means the dog was not having fun here.

Is she apprehensive, like aliens just landed?

Clarkson said: *"Not sure that apprehensive is right word, she seems disinterested. She showed the least amount of motivation with the toys (no food) covered up."*

Shows she did not learn to play alone or solve problems. Toys should be the puppy's laboratory to learn to cope with real life. Even though Bonnie is older, she can still be stimulated by providing and experimenting with various toys daily with toys that talk, squeak, squawk, are of differing textures etc.

Is she afraid? Does she run away?

Clarkson said: *"She left the room multiple times, but always came back."*

She is not afraid, just disinterested, seeing if she can find easier food. If she is not directed, she will always take the easy way, if that is the better choice to her. So impulse control will be something that you will want to add to her foundational skill work, plus adding regular play periods, foraging activities.

Does she lie down – where?

Clarkson said: *"She laid down opposite toys, she also laid on top. We have revisited mat training recently so this is her first response."*

As a trainer or canine pet guardian doing the CED, make sure you do write out your comments, what you learned from each step in the CED. It will open observable patterns. As a trainer working with a client on a CED, make sure you really listen and evaluate client comments and notice the patterns you are seeing.

The CED also helps the dog pet guardian to learn more about themselves in the process, and the trainer to learn more about their client so they can better coach the team and how that team learns. Some dog pet guardians simply do not enjoy interacting in play with their dogs, others love it.

Not only do we learn much needed information about the dog during a CED, but also about the pet guardian. It can make the difference between engaging, motivating and inspiring the pet guardian to work with their dog and through their issues. From this process with Bonnie a big piece to the puzzle emerged – impulse control.

When working with a guardian, trainers should relate back to other cases they've had or what they've done in their own families. It makes the learning real and personal for the client.

Valor with toy

For instance, my Belgian Tervuren, Valor, always gets a toy or treat coming through the doorway as he likes to showcase his mojo with the older males. The toy or treat redirection makes the door fun for him and the other dogs. Simple, not only does he automatically come through the door and pick up his toy, he finds a toy to take outdoors also. He generalized this task just from learning he would get a toy coming in through a door. This learned behavior continues even when no food is available.

Chapter 15

How the Dog Solves Problems

Problem-solving is different from toy play and active fetch games, as it uses the dog's mental power, their thinking skills to solve a problem. There is no readily, easy answer and some of the problems a dog may have never seen before. It requires interaction from their human and the hardest part for the pet guardian is to let the dog think once a problem is presented.

How a dog thinks through a problem, solves it, or does not solve it, says a lot about how they will solve a problem in real life. Problems that affect behavior.

How a dog sees the world

Tiring exercises in the CED include how the dog sees the world. An exercise on how they see color, and how they recognize size. There are also activities to involve scent and obstacle coursework to note equilibrium in movement, focus, fear of objects and how dog and pet guardian work as a team. The CED also looks at how the dog solves difficult problems. How the dog works through these mentally tiring activities shows us how they work through problems in real life, and even why they are reacting or aggressing and how to work through those issues.

In Day One there are two activities, one to test color recognition and the other, size recognition. One is completed in the morning and the other in the afternoon. This activity also tells a lot about how the pet guardian works with their dog, their patience level, their body cues, and how they help their dog to solve problems. It is not a right or wrong exercise but is to help tire the dog mentally so deep sleep comes readily. Yet, it also reveals a lot about how the dog sees their world, how they think things through or do not and it is for observation, not for obedience. See Chapter 14 for examples.

Lyn Dubois and her dog Tammy have a wonderful video of the advanced concept of size recognition. Concept of Tallest and Concept of smallest (https://www.youtube.com/watch?v=eIfHiiPAmW0)

- Basket Challenge – (https://www.youtube.com/watch?v=EKAbQpABtaw) a favorite

Max Basket Challenge

And games that use what a dog was naturally bred to do, like hunt,, retrieve, herd and so on. These exercises build confidence.

Photo 1 – Rusty with tunnel;

Photo 2 – Charlie with his rock

Rusty tunnels, while housemate Cocker Spaniel, Charlie retrieves.

Can Dogs See Color?

This is Annie, a Mexican Hairless mix, she nailed the right color every time no matter where it was put. She is aggressive to the other dogs in the household and really needed stress reduction. For two months after she went home, she was a different dog. Color choice is by recognition only, and a click/reward on correct find.

Dogs can clearly see yellow or blue, it is easier to find "by color". They have rods and cones in their eyes like what we do, however, they may distinguish color more as lighter tones, grays, blacks. They cannot see reds. Green looks white or light beige for instance. They see more grays in their line of sight. Yellows and blues are very distinguishable (in a lighter tone than we see them – but nonetheless – color). In this exercise, the observation is how dog sees color.

Questions to consider after this exercise:

- What egg or colored cup does he go to first.
- How does he approach the task – think about it?
- Does he move in too quickly making wrong decisions to find the food and not really looking at the color?
- Does he walk away to think? Do you let him think?
- Does he sometimes need more encouragement?
- OR does he really enjoy participation?

These observations affect how dog "thinks" and the process of behavior modification and even skill work. It also has a lot to say about personality and structuring a behavior modification program that works for the individual.

What happened when Bosco attempted the color recognition exercise?

Bosco, Miniature Pinscher

"Tried putting cup on a table but Bosco was nervous so moved to the floor. (**Showed creative thinking.**)

He doesn't seem to distinguish color but went more by either seeing me place the treat or by smell.(**Showed what he focuses on.**)

The entire exercise seemed to make him nervous and he displayed some avoidance signs, looking away, wandering off to grab things on the floor, looking out the window, etc. (**Bosco could have been "thinking" or "confused". Showed how he handles new information.**)

I aborted the exercise after just 3 or 4 trials with 2 cups. (**Shows good instincts to keep stress levels manageable, and keep Bosco successful.**)"

My reply in analysis: Again, this is just information. He may very well have been taxed by having to think about what was expected and probably got a few tries wrong. The displacement behaviors he did would be normal and sometimes a dog needs to move away to "think". We need to let them think. What I am learning about him is he quickly goes into fool around behavior which is a high-level stress behavior. He needs to feel very comfortable with learning activities. Less is more with him – i.e. short behavior modification sessions, short training sessions, keep sessions short and continue to work on the more advanced level click/treat exercise with the colored eggs. The point is to see how he thinks things through so you can keep this in mind when you do a behavior process with him, but also to mentally tire him so his head starts to feel heavy, his eyelids feel heavy, he just cannot stay awake and goes into a deep REM sleep. Teaching him to problem-solve is key to teaching him to make good decisions.

Guardian's update on Bosco July 21, 2014: "Bosco is doing really well. He is still very high drive, but I do not feel like I need to keep him constantly entertained anymore. The detox took the edge off his anxiety and over stimulation issues and he can now cuddle or play without getting the zoomies or being too rough."

Bosco's CED took place in February 2014. Update on Bosco February 19, 2015: " You should see how well Bosco is doing now. I still heat up his blanket in the dryer – he loves it!"

Bosco's Final Analysis looked like this: **Bosco's behavior modification protocol called for:**

Aversive motivator = triggers an object coming toward him

SUGGESTION: change it up and put object on a nearby table, call him over OR do S curves, an ARC to side versus "approaching directly to front" and watch his body language, allow him to make the choice to come to you.

Self-soothe Teaching

SUGGESTION: Give him something to do to occupy his mind, rather than just "wander around". Freeze stuffed Kongs; or empty marrow bones; or give him a big marrow bone – this will work his mouth and release tension. It will also tire him so he rests more deeply. He does not seem to know what to do with himself; how to self-soothe.

It seems to me he did not get the nurturing early on and give him appropriate things to suckle (use his mouth, release his muzzle tension); to grab and shake, rip, and tear and for nurturing, warmth, snuggling (even add a ticking clock or a sound machine that has a heart beat). You are taking him back to puppyhood and re- nurturing him.

Calming aids, alternative suggestions:

DAP diffuser ONLY in his resting spot and/or a bandanna with lavender or rescue remedy on it; on his bedding and collar.

Lactium is like mother's milk – give it to him before bedtime.

Also work for focus and to calm

Obstacle coursework in real life and around triggers can really ground him help him to be more focused and calm. – He really needs this. Drive to a spot and set up cones to weave through for instance, not quickly, slow, precise, meticulous, or a cavelletti or both. Walk him through a ladder on the ground; up steps on a walk; use the environment as it presents itself for an obstacle workout.

Functional Rewards – use premack principle with Bosco (esp. on walk/trains)

Sniffing

Allowing object grabbing – a cup, or trying a flirt pole

Safety Zone/Quiet Zone –

Bosco should be able to get away from distractions regularly, at first regulated and then "on his own accord". With routine of at least one hour safe zone, no distractions, dark, music on, warm and cozy (add a warm Thundershirt from the dryer versus wraps), then Bosco will start to look forward to this time and even seek it out himself.

Short sessions. (session – rest – session etc.)

He needs to feel very comfortable with learning activities, so **less is more** with him – i.e. short behavior modification sessions, short training sessions

Each dog is different in how they approach a problem. You can see here that some dogs become worried quickly, just by what we would think of as a simple learning experience. This affects how successful a behavior modification program will be and why. It breaks down into baby steps how this dog should be approaching learning situations to keep him successful and progressive.

Chai and The Size Exercise Example

Here is an example of the instructions for size recognition exercise. This was for a little dog named Chai who was experiencing anti-social behavior with people and other dogs, obsessive licking, growling/snapping. To the example below about the activity itself, any dog's name can be substituted.

Can Chai distinguish size? How does she handle changes in size? Important in evaluating how she relates to the environment and changes. See Chapter 14 for set up of size recognition exercise.

Depending on the individual, this game as done in this way might be too easy. To truly define if the dog is recognizing size versus using their nose, after the small container is completed successfully 80% of the time, then a clicker can be used and when small container is touched with the dog's nose, a reward is given OR the dog indicates with a nose touch which container is "small" and is given a reward for doing so. None of the other containers are rewarding.

This is the detail looked for when implementing a CED with a client dog or if a client attempts this on their own. The goal is to mentally tire the dog while learning about how they learn.

Problem Solving

Problem-solving activities in the CED satisfy what is natural for dogs to accomplish to avoid behavior issues. Dogs think, make decisions, good or bad, in response to the problem in front of them and what is going on in the environment. Dogs learn by association and consequence and default into what works to accomplish what they want. What they want in the activities is food reward. How they get it is to solve the problem in front of them and how they do so can help create a results-oriented behavior modification process postCED.

DIANE GARROD

Chapter 16

Deciphering the Physiology of Stress

"To understand the stress response, we must process a fundamental knowledge not only of psychology but of physiology as well."
- George Everly

The bad stress neurotransmitters are:

- Adrenalin (Epinephrine)
- Cortisol
- Neoepinephrine, and
- Noradrenalin

What is the purpose of these neurotransmitters?

How would you know if a dog was having an adrenalin rush? Adrenalin (or Epinephrine) is a hormone produced by the adrenal glands. Adrenalin triggers **fight, flight** response and outwardly evidence will be seen as a dog who is:

- overly-energetic
- extremely alert
- and digestive system shuts down resulting in the dog can't take treats

The Body prepares for war, for survival.

Adrenalin

Adrenalin is also released when there is stress but no actual danger. The dog perceives danger and becomes restless and irritable and removing or redirecting the dog becomes necessary.

What happens when there are high levels of adrenalin? High levels of adrenalin can lead to chronic stress, which becomes evident when the dog has insomnia, which means the dog is unable to retain serotonin reserves or build melatonin. The dog will be pacing, whining, biting, have OCD (obsessive compulsive disorder) behaviors and will not be able to relax. What you know is that stress release must occur for behavior modification to be successful and lasting. Exercise is one way to use up this extra energy, but not if the exercise itself is stressful. The CED process is now another way. And understanding that exercise that releases stress is preferable to that which increases stress. Examples of stress releasing exercise is where dog has zero reactions on a walk, they have fun playing Frisbee, or having fun in dog sports with positive performance results. This is the good stress created by the good experiences in life. This is where you will see a natural, healthy, heavy or deep sleep after what the dog loves to do versus increased reactivity or aggression due to heightening a dog's senses in a bad way from distress.

Eustress or good stress, is the feel good stress, while distress, the feel bad type of stress, can lead to chronic/acute stress. An example would be that a dog is:

- fearful about a situation,
- or dog is in a panic or
- in pain

What will you see to tip off that the dog is stressed?

- lack of relaxation
- fighting relaxation and
- even health issues

The Physiology Basics

It does not have to be complex to understand what goes on inside the dog's body. When stress hormones are released they either go to the sympathetic nervous system or create endorphins which release or decrease pain.

The sympathetic nervous system (SNS)

The sympathetic nervous system (SNS) is part of the autonomic nervous system (ANS). It is responsible for activating fight or flight response operating through a series of interconnected neurons considered a part of the peripheral nervous system (PNS). Many of these neurons also lie within the central nervous system (CNS). Sympathetic neurons release acetylcholine, a chemical messenger.

In response to this stimulus, noradrenalin (norepinephrine) is released. Prolonged activation can elicit the release of adrenaline from the adrenal medulla. This is what causes fight or flight.

One would know when this occurs because pupil dilation, increased sweating, and increased heart rate would occur as outward signs.

Once stress goes into the sympathetic nervous system through the autonomic nervous system it disperses and becomes either norepinephrine involving sympathetic nerves OR epinephrine (adrenalin) involving the adrenal medulla, If norepinephrine is involved this is when increases in heart rate will be seen and what we can't see is lipid breakdown and peripheral vasoconstriction increasing plasma fatty acids available for energy.

If stress is prolonged it will take the path of an adrenalin rush (epinephrine). In addition to heart rate increase, lipid breakdown, and peripheral vasoconstriction, the dog's body will also experience coronary and bronchial dilation, muscle and liver glycogen and glucose release, which increases serum glucose causing increased energy with no place to go. It makes sense that it will come out in reactivity or aggression as a result.

Cortisol

Cortisol is a glucocorticoid and essential for life (as discussed in Chapter One). It is naturally released in conditions of:

- stress,
- infection,

- pain,
- surgery or
- trauma

The ugly news is that in excess cortisol poisons the dog's body, and on the flip side, if there is not enough cortisol problems also occur as seen below.

- Cushings Disease – caused by an EXCESS balance of cortisol
- Addison's Disease – caused by a LOW balance of cortisol

And yet, Cortisol is needed to sustain life and maintain important body functions.

Neoepinephrine

Neoepinephrine is also released in the adrenal gland. Active neoepinephrine will cause:

- Increases in heart rate
- Increases in respiration (normal is up to 34 breaths per minute)
- Increases in blood pressure
- Increases in metabolism

Blood vessels open wider to let more blood flow to the large muscle groups, like legs and back, putting muscles on alert. Liver releases some stored glucose and glycogen to increase energy. What is then seen outwardly in the dog is pupil dilation to improve vision, the production of sweat to cool the body (panting, foot pads), and causes reactivity swiftly and effectively to handle a perceived threat.

High norepinephrine and epinephrine (or adrenalin) levels result in fight or flight in humans and canines.

Noradrenalin or Norepinephrine

Noradrenalin or norepinephrine is a cousin to adrenalin (see further explanation above under section titled sympathetic nervous system).

Function is different with noradrenalin acting as a neurotransmitter and creating a role in the dog's outward:

- Alertness
- Arousal

Stress and Aggression

A Zaragoza University study in Spain reported in the journal of Applied Animal Behavior Sciences took blood samples from 80 dogs aggressive toward humans . They compared the blood samples to those taken from non-aggressive dogs. The aggressive dogs averaged 278 units of serotonin (the mood enhancing neurotransmitter), while the others had 387.

The aggressive dogs also had high levels of cortisol, averaging 21 units compared to 10 in the non- aggressive dogs

These findings by the Zaragoza team conclusively back up the theory that maintaining an appropriate level of serotonin and cortisol is important to maintaining impulse control and reducing aggression. This leads us to the feel good neurotransmitters.

The feel good neurotransmitters

What should stress release accomplish? it should activate the feel good neurotransmitters of:

- Serotonin"
- Oxytocin
- Dopamine
- Endorphins

Serotonin

Serotonin's main duty is that it affects mood and happiness. Serotonin is a neurotransmitter that plays an intricate role in the way a dog eats, sleeps, and behaves. Level changes in serotonin equals behavior changes will occur. Increased stress levels often lead to mild or moderate depression, indicating serotonin levels are in low reserve. This increased stress level and resulting decrease in serotonin level can be a cause of canine aggression. High levels of serotonin in people result in happiness and love while low levels of serotonin result in depression.

Oxytocin

Oxytocin is the feel good chemical, creating feelings of love and a sense of well-being. New research findings on Oxytocin show reductions in:

- anxiety states,
- stress,
- addictions, (such as OCD behaviors, excessive barking)
- problems of birth in breeding programs

Building oxytocin happens through toy/games, problem-solving, and physical contact, relationship building exercises during the CED.

Dopamine

Pleasure seeking feeling when engaged in activities enjoyed such as when a border collie is engaged in herding describe in detail the evolved motor patterns in various types of dogs – livestock guardians, heelers, hounds, pointers and retrievers.

Dopamine is a double-edged sword because this same system is a powerhouse behind extreme pleasure-seeking activities (i.e. fence chasing, car chasing, over-barking can all release a dopamine rush). In humans, high dopamine levels can result in schizophrenia, while low dopamine levels result in anxiety and depression.

Endorphins

Endorphins are like the natural pharmacy of the body and work with sedative receptors that are known to relieve common pain. Endorphins are not a single molecule, but actually come in several forms, and can be anywhere from eighteen to five hundred times as powerful as any man-made analgesic, and is non-addictive.

Endorphins are released through exercise. We all know the dog whose pain seems to go away when they are doing something they love. This is the body at work protecting them through the release of endorphins.

Endorphins are morphine-like, indicated in the name, endogenous + morphine. Endorphins are small, protein molecules that are produced by cells in the nervous system.

How Does the CED Work to Release Stress

Stress release is a part of working with the dog from the inside out. The CED works with a dog's natural senses of smell, taste, hearing, vision, and touch. It introduces non-habituated feelings throughout the body and creates new habits. It creates new, stimulating ways of thinking while helping to understand how the dog might perceive real life, which can give insight into how and why they react the way they do. The CED ends up neutralizing bad stress chemicals in brain and body.

I love that it (the CED) truly prepares the dog to begin a behavior modification plan, as well as giving the trainer lots of valuable information about the dog. Vicki Aquino Ronchette, Braveheart Dog Training, San Leandro, CA, USA

Prepares is a suitable word as the CED helps gather valuable information, not just about the dog), but about their environment and pet guardians and, at the same time, the CED is fun and specific; it reveals specifics about each dog as an individual.

How a dog thinks, responds or does not and how they problem-solve are revealed in a CED and helps pull the pieces together that make up the final analysis (behavior modification program). Here are a few examples:

Wally deeply sleeping during his CED

In this video of Wally (https://www.youtube.com/watch?v=BFLsMey-gI6I), a case of extreme fear, showing how an obstacle course can help build confidence when the dog is ready. It can also show areas where the dog is not yet ready and gives a good look at body language and movement.

Close up interactivity and focus on the dog as an individual is a side benefit of the CED for dog pet guardians, fosters, and trainers. The pet guardian's encouragement allows Wally to handle his stress and to pass the videographer without worry. This was important in his rehabilitation process. For the companion dog pet guardians, rescuers reading this book, making note of these subtleties takes the CED to the next level. Wally is also portrayed in Bernie Seigel's book "Love, Animals and Miracles". Today, Wally can function quite normally, loves the outdoors, takes treats from people, and progresses daily in his fears.

If Wally could talk he would tell it like it is "*I run at the beach, I return to my person, I play with other dogs, I take treats from people I do not know. I let some selected humans pet me. I am engaged in a happy dog's life. I learned how to do all these things with my support group at Canine Transformation's (Confident Transformations)classes. They are all my family!*"

A May 2015 update from Wally's pet guardian:

"Wally's journey has been amazing. Patience, love, and lots of encouragement under the guiding hand and heart of Diane with Canine Transformation taught Wally not all humans will hurt him. Diane's wealth of knowledge and support helped carry me through the often very difficult times." Lynn K., Whidbey Island, Washington

Quinn, Australia

Another example in evaluating how a dog problem-solves is the basket exercise. In this video (https://www.youtube.com/watch?v=Vbk6jNDs-RVc&feature=youtu.be) Chihuahua Quinn problem-solvingto figure out where the treats are and on which cloth, a connectivity exercise.

The goal is to pull the correct cloth that has the treat on it with mouth or dig it out with paws. The observation is how does he think the problem through? This tells a lot about how he processes information. His pet guardian sets him up for success in the video, gives him a clear cue, and allows him to think.

Often, as dog pet guardians we want to manipulate our canine companions and give them very little opportunity to think through problems on their own, to use their mental faculties, their brain. You can view how eager Quinn is to participate and he looks over the options and solves the problem. Quinn was a dog who can learn to solve his behavioral issues (who was dog reactive, worried about people in high distraction areas and hyperactive) and has with clear direction and attention and allowing him to think, set him up for success. Praise at the end indicates, "yes, you did the right thing." The look on Quinn's face is priceless.

May 2015 update from his pet guardian:

"Quinn continues to improve since finishing his first CED over a year ago. I love the program not only what it does for dogs but also for pet guardians. The insight it gives us is incredible. I am much more mindful now of how stress chemicals build up in us all and how that can make it virtually impossible for us to not react - as much as it is impossible for a boiling kettle not to let off steam. This gives me a much better understanding of how to support and understand Quinn's behavior. From a chihuahua who would take off over a large expanse to do that horrid bark and nip at other dogs, we now have no trouble being out and about where other dogs are present. In fact Quinn is a regular demo dog for K9 Nose Work at fairs and different dog events. To have him be able to work happily and confidently when he is surrounded by sometimes hundreds of other dogs is mind blowing. It only goes to show what we can do for these animals when we know what to do. Diane's work is pivotal in making so many dogs and pet guardians life better. Quinn and I are lucky to be amongst them." Peta Clarke, Australia

Chai notebook

In this video of Chai (https://www.youtube.com/watch?v=rUSM6Yx-i8gs) you have a comparison of responses in the same thinking game as Quinn is completing. Chai has a much different response to it, and not thinking it through is also an observation that affects a behavior modification program. It can indicate fear, confusion, social deficits and more. You see Chai turn her head and appear to be ignoring the basket altogether. This indicates she has not had to use her mind, or she is fearful of objects or she may have had a bad experience and is in avoidance. She is fearful and worried about what might happen. This is how she will approach behavior modification process.

In a second try video of Chai (https://www.youtube.com/watch?v=Xgs-FpVwf_qE), initially you see avoidanceagain, head turn, low body. In this exercise, pet guardians are asked to say cue once and let their dog think beyond that cue. The cue points to the basket and Chai is visibly worried, she avoids the basket, tiptoes around it, does a stressful round of displacement sniffing and redirects her attention the cat. She avoids the exercise altogether. This is usually the case with dogs who react intensely, who are unsure and worried, cautious and it means a lot of groundwork needs to be laid prior to addressing any serious behavior issues.

There were many positive outcomes for Chai from the CED:

- More responsive
- Ended licking without being told
- Going to her bed while pet guardians were eating without being asked
- Starting to really relax
- Finding a toy she can forage with and loves to enjoy, releasing mouth tension and anxiety
- Discovered Thundershirt worked well
- Non-reactive walk
- Better handling and voice tones

A January 2015 update from Chai's pet guardians stated:

"Today is Chai's 5th birthday and I was enjoying what that meant—AND what a contribution you made to our lives with your help. She is a different dog today. Happily, I can say that after three months we fully weaned her off the Prozac utilizing the help of our Bach Flower Essences expert while we decreased the dosage. She is still Chai --with her terrier traits and personality based on her early life (and karma?) but she is not the emotionally tormented pup when we first contacted you. Just wanted to thank you for all you did of us and for what you do for others."

Chapter 17

The Golden Nugget, The Final Analysis

If you've come this far, you've completed the CED and now it's time to pull together all the information gathered. The Final Analysis uses canine analysis and science to show the patterns that emerge during a CED and how to interpret them. It is the first step to create the first stages of a behavior modification program. It helps ease into a behavior modification and skills applications process and is progressive and results-oriented. It is the golden nugget to the CED process and needs the eye of a skilled trainer.

Each dog is an individual and so each Final Analysis is individualized based on what was learned over three days of the CED (analysis of video, photos, and guardian comments). While dogs learn the same, through association and consequences, they do not think the same, have the same perceptions or have the same personalities.

Understanding how a dog thinks helps create a BCP (behavior modification program) that will be results- oriented. It is modern cognitive ethology (Ethos = observation), the study of cognitive (thinking) processing in animals. This is done through perception exercises in color and size recognition in the CED (*see chapter 13, 14 and 15*). The dog must problem-solve, think, remember. Therefore, learning and memory are used in foraging and intelligence games, as well as in toy play coupled with the decision making properties of problem-solving activities.

What are the definitions of cognition?

Cognition refers to thought processes, consciousness, emotions, beliefs, and rationality in animals based on Darwinian continuity. Cognition refers to the mechanisms by which animals acquire, process, stare and act on information from the environment.

This is where toys/games, problem-solving (*as viewed in Chapters 13, 14* and 15) becomes important in analyzing the guardian's comments and resulting final analysis. Using what is discovered in a life-changing behavior modification and skills training system includes prevention, management, and supervision protocols. This helps to shorten the process of changing emotional responses and making it longer lasting.

A CED Final Analysis can be several pages long, longest was 70 pages in a very complicated case. Final Analysis can range from 10 to 35 pages on average. Each analysis postCED is individualized, so no two are exactly the same. It contains a graph at the beginning to help dog guardian work through process systematically to change behavior. This Final Analysis becomes the behavior modification process, This is where trainer uses their professional observation and analysis skills to decipher the CED and customize a behavior modification process. in addition to the behavior modification process or a guideline for the dog guardian to work through. It is an important part of the CED and what makes progress continuous postCED.

Short List of Categories to Use in FInal Analysis

- A Review of Biologics over three days
- Health and Nutrition Concerns
- Handling Tips for Guardian
- Behavior Modification and Skills Analysis (where they are now, where they want to be, how they will get there)
- Stress Release and Calming Exercises
- Confidence Building

All would be customized to the individual and also include their stress signals and a synopsis of their personality. In the Final Analysis you are looking for patterns and sorting out what the core behavior might be to help change emotional responses through a focused behavior modification process. Add other categories as needed.

Thank you Chancellor for coming into my life.
Many dogs will lead better lives.

Painting by Lynda McCormick, Freeland, WA.

Appendix 1

INTAKE FORM SAMPLE

Note to trainers – *add or delete questions as appropriate to your specific business*

1) Today's Date

2) Your Name:

3) Your Mailing Address

Street:

City, State, Zip:

Home Phone:

Work Phone:

e-mail address:

Occupation:

Names, ages, and genders of other family members:

Occupations of other family members:

Please describe your and your family's pet owning experience:

Treated pet's name:

Treated pet's breed:

Treated pet's gender:

Treated pet's age:

Spay/neuter: What age?

Age at which you obtained this pet:

Veterinarian:

Phone:

Current diet and food intake:

Diet history/troubles with food:

Medication history:

Chronic health problems:

Please describe any injuries or surgeries:

Early history if known: i.e. birth conditions, litter size, sibling sexes, temperament and health of parents, temperament of other family members, amount of human or animal contact, early rearing experiences, traumatic events, health and emotional state when brought into your home, etc. –

Name, species, gender, age, and spay/neuter status of any other pets in the household:

Current level of physical activity:

Are walks stress free? If not, why not?

Reason for acquiring this animal:

Reason you are seeking treatment/training:

Top three behaviors to be addressed:

Do the stress levels or emotional states of the animal's housemates seem to affect the animal's behavior? Describe:

Is s/he sound sensitive? High or low frequencies? Paper rustling? Squeaks? Buzzers? Fireworks, gun shots, automobile backfires? If so, do sounds send him/her into a 'state'? What does s/he do – panic and hide, kick into chase/prey drive, bite, bark, whine, spin, chew on him/herself, etc.?

Is s/he touch sensitive? Does s/he allow you to trim nails, clean ears & teeth, etc. Does he/she like to be petted? If not, why not, what does he/she do?

Is s/he motion sensitive? How does s/he react to objects or animals moving quickly?

Does s/he travel well? How does s/he travel: crate, back seat, trailer, RV etc.? Does s/he pace, whine cry, freeze, become ill in cars or confinement?

When is s/he happiest and most relaxed? What activities does s/he like?

When is s/he most anxious? What things or activities are his/her least favorite?

Is s/he afraid of strange people? Explain in detail please. Does s/he display fear around any familiar people? How does s/he display this?

Does s/he fight or flee or freeze or fool around when afraid? Does this animal have a bite history? Explain exactly what bites looked like, photos if possible and exactly what occurred before the bite, during the bite, and after the bite. (Use back of this page to explain in detail)

How does s/he handle vet visits?

How is s/he with other animals? (dogs, cats, birds, bunnies, squirrels) Explain in detail. Describe his/her behavior around unknown animals or people? How does s/he display this?

What is his/her apparent position in the family? Are there ever struggles or friction?

How would you describe his/her personality and temperament? (Here are some examples of what others have said: "party animal", "kamikaze", "afraid of his/her own shadow", "loner", "aloof", "disconnected", "social butterfly", "ready for action", "ADHD", "Hair Trigger", "Couch Potato", "Pushy", "Depressed", "lap dog" etc.

How many hours per day indoors….& outside?

Anything unique or unusual about his/her behavior or temperament? You've described a lot about behavior problems already, however, here is a place to make additions, after thoughts, or get into more detail (i.e. has killed rabbits, fowl, deer and eaten them; has a bite including any "bruising"). Please do not leave anything out here and use as much space as you need for all the questions.

For how long has the animal's behavior or health been a concern? Did this issue arise suddenly or following an experience? Please describe:

1. What types of collar(s) and leash(es) do you currently use? Why?

2. What books/videos/television and other resources have you referred to in order to educate yourself about dogs and dog training? Are these venues fear and force free?

3. Have you ever sought help for this issue previously? If so, with whom and for how long? What were the results?

4. What is wonderful about your dog?

Appendix 2

CANINE EMOTIONAL DETOX – CLIENT PREPARATION LIST

Preferably dog issues already or beginning; sound sensitivities; erosion of relationship in households; also, for the normal distressed, anxious dog and dogs with health issues

NOTE TO TRAINERS (do not put this NOTE in your client packet): Additions or deletions occur based on behavior. Extreme fear and dogs who cannot be touched for instance, take out touch and be creative adding a feather for touch, or a Ttouch wand wrapped with ace bandage at one end. Further improvisation may include minimal husbandry or no husbandry (no bath or dry bath; etc.). Separation anxiety challenges would include increased foraging activity working with moving pet guardian out of room while dog is hunting for food to prepare for next steps. Biters can provide an exercise in DS & CC movement for example. Noise and object sensitivities can provide incremental sound increases via YouTube or DVD of noise dog is sensitive to, or slow exposure to an object. Improvise as needed, make additions and deletions appropriate to the behavior you are seeing in intake form and/or a functional assessment.

Over three days –

NOTE: I may add or delete items as customized to each dog's challenges. However, this is a general list of items you will need to begin.

RELAXERS

- ☐ Warm towel – from dryer OR Blanket (muscle relaxant) – A sensory exercise

- ☐ Thundershirt, if you have one OR Ace bandages (work just as well and sometimes better) – 2 – one 2″ and one 1 " – can be found at any pharmacy – make sure you don't get the "sticky ones" – Velcro is ideal.

☐ Shampoo = dog shampoo – preferably one with a chamomile, lavender, or other relaxing agent OR a DRY bath available at pet stores (no bath if dog is extremely fearful, a biter)

NOT A RELAXER. Sensory COLD – Ice cubes (with a berry in the middle if you have berries) – how she handles "cold" – can prepare these ahead now – if you do not have berries other fruit is fine. I test warmth and cold. We will put ice "on dog and "see how they handle this internally and externally. Some dogs prefer cold to warm. Some dogs do find cold relaxing, especially those with high respiration, who heat up quickly when they are not exercising, and it is not hot outside.

INTERNAL DETOX/ELIMINATION DIET – FOOD – no regular (kibbled) food throughout the 3 days. Why? This is to allow the dog's system to detox from the inside out – an elimination cleanse – as well as their emotional level/stress levels, and to see how they are processing their food. ONE MEAT SOURCE – organic preferred, no antihistamines, hormones etc. (i.e., chicken or turkey or halibut COOKED or RAW – these meats contain tryptophan in varying amounts a natural relaxant, but more importantly they are easily available). Please let me know what you choose, and all the supplements dog is currently taking, if any. BUT NO KIBBLE. No offal, no organs, no eggs for now. Keep current on meds.

TREATS: Use the one protein source for treats – i.e., chicken (make extra).

IN ADDITION TO PROTEIN.

FIBER (to move things through the digestive system) Brown rice or quinoa, pumpkin or steel cut oatmeal OR PUMPKIN (brown rice is more nutrient dense than white and white can spike sugar levels – also rice can ferment in the system). Amount based on dog's weight: from 1/8 to 1/2 cup for small/medium dogs 2X per day; to 1 to 3 cups for medium to extra-large dogs 2X a day – of each protein and fiber. Meat can be cooked or raw.

LOTS of treats – recommending "no preservatives" – so turkey, liver, or organic dog treats – no salt, no sugar, no soy, no grains (allow 1/4 cup for exercises daily). Can go "pure" and stick with turkey or even use the Country Pet as treats.

DAY TWO: add carrots portion 1/8 to 1/2 cup depending on dog's weight (you will serve these warm, fresh, organic carrots) – food processor or liquify (served warm) – otherwise they will not be able to digest them easily. Sensory exercise – sweet taste.

DAY THREE: broccoli or brussel sprouts, green beans – cooked – in day three – food processor or liquify – 1/2 cup INSTEAD of carrots. Sensory exercise – sour taste.

NO hot dogs, NO cheese, peanut butter treats, NO tuna brownies, NO preservatives, grains (except for the carb you choose above) and no dairy of any kind.

probiotic tablet or capsule (again to cleanse system) – available at pet store (you may already be giving this). (optional) Esp. important if dog is on medication as meds destroy the good bacteria in the gut. The probiotic maintains the good bacteria. At the very least plain yogurt or Greek yogurt is acceptable.

ACTIVITY NEEDS – may add more here.

- [ ] Three plastic cups – neutral color – small, medium, and large
- [ ] Five different colored cups or easter eggs (plastic type) – must contain one yellow, one blue.
- [ ] Equipment – sticks (broom, mop, or other sticks for cavelletti); cones or buckets; and anything else you might have on hand to do obstacle workout, small agility course work.
- [ ] Toys (cardboard box to put toys in or formal toy box with lid) – variety.
- [ ] Strips of cloth, a laundry basket or bicycle basket (off the bike) or other see-through type of basket

ALONE TIME – relaxing, calming to promote deep sleep.

- [ ] A place where relaxation is undisturbed. This is a place they feel safe and it CAN be with you.

☐ Relaxation MUST NOT BE FORCED. Each dog must willingly give in to relaxation – no cues to lie down – you just provide the distraction free, comfortable place for maximum stress release.

☐ A quiet NO DISTRACTION place to sleep/relax alone – I do proof separation anxiety in this detox (invisible dog exercise)

☐ Music – classical, or "Through a Dog's Ear" made for dogs or any soft, mellow music is good. MUST be "relaxing" music and preferably made for dogs.

A NOTE ABOUT WALKS – IF THE WALK is stressful – NO WALKS during the three days. There will be plenty of activity to substitute and physical stimulation. IF THE WALK is enjoyed, then a brief awareness walk will be provided BUT please tell me your thoughts on this piece, because if we are neutralizing stress, we do not want stress to rebuild if a dog is seen on a walk.

GROOMING TOOLS – bond time

☐ Brush

☐ Nail clipper, dreml or nail file

MUST have digital camera for photos, video capability. VIDEO: :30 to 1:30 tops. Digitals should be jpeg or gif. Can add to these files to a FREE service www.dropbox.com. All you must do is invite me in (via garrod@ whidbey.com) to view your files.

COMMIT to do the CED exactly as written, AND for best results.

TRAINERS – ADDITIONAL REQUIREMENTS – for more detail in CED Final Analysis

CED REQUIREMENT LIST – to check prior to CED and to get a comparison value in day three. **Note:** these are checks (biologics) any pet guardian can and should do regularly to check the health of their dog. It helps greatly when taking dog to veterinarian and presenting vet with more specific information about a dog's health. During CED it helps to analyze whether behavior might be due to any of these elements. Do not guess, KNOW.

- **Resting respiratory rate** (up to 34 normal) https://www.youtube. com/watch?v=uEptzj6G-Jk

- **Temperature** (if you have that or last reading from you chart at the vet), **Day One and Day Three** https://www.youtube.com/ watch?v=cXjg77ShJbM HOW TO https://www.youtube.com/ watch?v=3z8ptw3Qj5g WHAT IS NORMAL?

- **Weight** (or last recorded weight from vet and date taken) – taken daily – day one baseline sometimes a dog can lose a lb. during the detox diet and that means we need to increase the food – can watch this too by satiation levels – or decrease if food is left and so on – very important.

- **Waste photo** – day one morning AND then day three morning

- **Check gums** and report a) red or b) pink or c) pale white.

One of the first things a vet might ask before you take a dog to the emergency room is the color of the gums. Gums that are lighter or darker than normal can indicate several problems requiring medical attention. In general, a healthy dog has pink gums. "If gums are pale, the cause can be internal bleeding — especially common in older, large-breed dogs — or it can be due to low blood pressure or low body temperature. Bright-red gums can be caused by a fever and an infection."

Check pH balance – urine strip – inexpensive and available at any pharmacy or online

DURING CED will be looking also at:

Legs and Paws Your dog should always bear weight **equally on all four legs**. Both sprains and bone cancer can show up as "light lameness." You will check for lumps and bumps (during husbandry portion of the CED), particularly paying close attention in older large-breed dogs. Asymmetry in the legs can suggest a disease that involves withering of the muscles.

A dog's paws are vulnerable to contact dermatitis, and dogs usually lick their paws repeatedly to manage the irritation. Excessive redness between the toes can mean that either a bacterial or yeast infection has set in. All can have an irritability effect making behavior issues heighten. In the CED, you will walk your dog up and back towards the camera naturally, and go over an obstacle course noting how the dog moves, carries themself etc.

Eyes Eyes should be bright and clear. The whites are white, and there is no discharge. In contrast, less-than-healthy eyes are red and may be a notable source of irritation. Redness can indicate anything from dry eye to glaucoma to an infectious disease. Discharge may be suggestive of an eye ulcer. The color recognition exercise also serves as an "eye test" of sorts while also evaluating how your dog thinks.

Ears Healthy ears are reasonably clean and do not smell bad. The floppy part is neither pink nor red. Also, both ears should look the same on the inside. If there is a difference, the animal may have either a bacterial or a yeast infection.

Abundant earwax can also signify an ear infection. "If your dog is scratching at its ears a lot, check the wax. Normal earwax is pale gray to light brown and is not abundant.

Skin and Hair Ideally, your dog's skin is pink, without patchy areas of hair loss or irritation. Your dog should smell like a dog. With some skin diseases, the dog will smell yeasty or stinky. Excessive skin scratching is another way your dog may alert you to skin issues.

A healthy canine coat has luster. You can see if a dog's hair is healthy, just like you can with a person. Hair should not have a lot of dander and should not feel greasy. Abundant hair loss can indicate anything from anxiety to endocrine disease and nutritional deficits. The CED will point out nutrition areas, suggestions, tips.

Teeth Dental health is as important in dogs as in people. Good dental hygiene shows up in your dog's breath as well as its teeth. Dog pet guardians are surprisingly reluctant to investigate their dogs' mouths, however, doing so is important, as dental disease is common — especially in small dogs, which tend to have longer life spans.

Teeth are a potential source of pain and infection. Monitoring dog's breath and the amount of tartar on its teeth is important. When either takes a turn for the worse, it may be time for a cleaning to prevent more serious problems down the road.

All the above might indicate it is time for a vet check, a chiropractic exam, an eye test etc. Much of the above could be responsible for behavioral changes and challenges in a dog. They are all important to the CED. Stress release occurs quickly in a healthy body. You want to do away with abnormal spikes and levelling out and see more eustress (the good stress) and stress spikes appropriate to context that come down quickly.

Appendix 3

PERMISSION FORM SAMPLE

Photo/Video Permission slip

Permission is requested to use any photos/videos/testimonials/comments on the Canine Transformations Learning Center (cTLC) website, books (where appropriate), Facebook case study, speaking engagements and presentations, and in marketing materials.

Pictures and videos will not be sold.

Photos/videos will be used exclusively for our cTLC promotional purposes, and as regards the subject matter.

_____ Yes, I give permission for photographs and/or video of my dog to be used in the above format.

_____ Yes, _____ No I do or do not give permission for photographs and/or video of me, my voice, or my name to be used in the above format. If you wish only a certain format of your name to be used and not address, but allow city or state, please indicate below.

_____ No, I do not give permission for my dog or myself to be photographed and/or videotaped for cTLC promotional purposes as indicated in first paragraph.

_____

Name(s) of dog(s)

Appendix 4

CED LIABILITY FORM SAMPLE

Canine Emotional Detox – Liability Form

I hereby acknowledge that I have voluntarily applied to participate in the Canine Emotional Detox: Stress release protocol for challenging canines with (name of business and name of one conducting CED).

I hereby waive all claims or actions that I or my family or my guardians or representatives may have, from all personal injury to myself, my dog, children in my charge, or harm to property or person caused directly or indirectly, through action or inaction of self or others, by acts that might occur in the duration of the CED, without trainer present or engaged.

I agree to indemnify (name of business here) and its employees and affiliates from all claims by myself, member of family, or any agent in conjunction with the CED, or incidents within my home property, or in the public because of any action or inaction, of either my dog or any another.

I also agree to assume sole responsibility for injury or damage caused by myself, children in my charge, or by the dog I own or handle and further agree to indemnify, defend, and hold the instructors, trainers, assistants, and property harmless from any damage, loss, liability, or expense, including legal cost and attorney's fees, which result from damage caused by myself, children in my charge, or by the dog I own or handle.

I have read the policies for conducting the Canine Emotional Detox (CED) and I agree to adhere to them. The CED is a systematic process and I agree to follow it step-by-step as written, to comment and to present video and photos as required.

Dog Pet guardian Signature _____

Trainer Participants, if applicable (each sign)_____

Other team members must sign (if pertinent, vet, vet bah, canine nutrition expert, etc.) _____

Appendix 5

DAY ONE EXAMPLE

Since Day One is based on behavior seen in intake form and/or functional assessment. Additions and deletions should occur based on preparation list and follow-up note at top. You can formulate your client document from this, use your own client photos and photo descriptions, personalize it. Use the protocol cycle as your guide.

Canine Emotional Detox/De-stress (CED)

(description of behavior goes here)

(dog's name and date of CED go here)

DAY ONE – STAGE ONE – Goal:

- complete relaxation
- coupled with intense, short activity bursts
- camera ready?
- items on list on hand?

START: REMEMBER, you are working from **the inside out** with (dog's name here) and how she starts her day determines the rest of the day – so commit **to zero distraction, zero reactivity**. (NOTE: If you do have a reaction – not just an alert bark, but an OVER-reaction, describe it – time of day, where, what, who etc.).

BEFORE BREAKFAST

- potty first
- evaluate poo (what does it look like, does (dog's name) strain, what color, consistency is it? take a photo of it – I know – gross!)

T-TOUCH: Do a BELLY LIFT BEFORE BREAKFAST

Belly lift photo – technique. Place ace bandage just after last rib. Gently stretch moving straight up with both hands (without lifting dog off feet – this is a very gentle exercise) for a soft count of three. As you do INHALE.

Release slowly to a count of three, EXHALE. REPEAT 3 times. Use a 1″ wrap for dog (this is for smaller dog). 3X means from back of ribs as 1; mid-belly as 2; and just behind back thighs as 3. Slowly, gently. Why? This helps relax the stomach, moves through any waste stuck and starts the cleansing process. It is a gentle process – gently, barely felt upward and gently, barely seen by human eye – that gentle – but felt by the dog.

BREAKFAST

Food for the next three days will be a mild cleansing diet as discussed in the PREP LIST. Choose ONE meat source. NOTE: You may need to adjust portions up or down depending on consumption and satiation. Each meal.

AFTER BREAKFAST ANSWER THESE QUESTIONS

- Is she still hungry afterwards?
- Does she eat?
- Is she satisfied?

DIGESTION RELAXATION

NEXT: 20 minutes after eating a full relax period – no distractions, no excitement (either in a room, or a crate, or on the couch or a mat – she must rest) – then potty break again and poo evaluation (IF NO POO GOTTEN IN THE FIRST MORNING RUN). Compare poos, or just say there was none etc. NOTE: It takes 20 minutes for food to digest and move through system. How a dog digests their food is important part of the emotional detoxification.

- A dog's stomach will work on breaking down food for approximately eight hours before passing it into the small intestine.
- The broken-down food will remain in the intestine for about two days, depending on how difficult it is to break it down.
- Whatever remains when small intestines are finished is passed to the large intestine and processed in a few hours.
- References: Vet Info; Washington State University

BENEFITS of DIGESTIVE DETOXIFICATION

Cleans out body waste deposits, so dog is not running with a dirty engine or functioning with the brakes on. This is where the belly lift really helps to move things along and to relax dog.

- Dogs behavior starts to change because actual cell make-up has changed.
- Digestive tract is cleansed of accumulated waste and fermenting bacteria.
- Excess mucous and congestion is cleared from body. Therefore, I need to see the waste.
- Mental clarity is enhanced, impossible under chemical overload.
- Resource Linda Page N.D., PhD

FIRST SENSORY ACTIVITY

WARMTH. Then recreate warmth, this time with a soft, fluffy towel from the dryer – for the release of muscle tension and stress. **(Do Ttouch and a ½ wrap (attached handout on how to do the wrap) with this sensory application.)** If your Thundershirt has arrived, you can use that – it must be put on tightly – the pressure is what causes the relaxation. DO NOT USE AS A JACKET. Calm, relaxation must be taught, just as a sit must be taught – they are just differing types of education.

RELAXATION 1 full hour – wrap or Thundershirt OFF.

HOW THE MORNING STARTS sets the tone for the whole rest of the day.

Activity, learning, education

Should be ABOUT mid-morning BUT time of day is not as important as completion of each exercise as written performing the RIGHT COMBINATION criteria.

PLAY

Play is so important for dogs as it is for kids – this is their laboratory where they try things out.

Mid-morning. Look at this as an educational phase, as you first learn HOW DOGPLAYS ALONE. No talking or encouraging, just watching, and observing.

First five minutes – just put stuff down, sit on floor or on a chair and observe.

Next five minutes – hide two or three toys under a cloth or blanket and go back and sit down.

Last five minutes – take some pre-prepared treats that were discussed in the LIST and hide in under or IN some toys and pile them all up.

At end of time. Throw up your hands, look at dog and say, "that'll do!" (or any release word just so it is consistent and indicates we are done). Look away and pick up all the toys and put them away (no toy left on the floor of your house anywhere and put them up high). WHY? Because the play becomes more valuable to dog – it doesn't equal boring toys scattered all over, it indicates YES, I can't wait to see what toys we'll play with today. AND it makes you more valuable, more worth listening to. You become FUN not confrontational.

ANSWER THESE QUESTIONS

- Is she creative?
- Does she have fun?

YOUR ROLE here is to put down a pile of toys and evaluate what dog does for a full 15 minutes with no help from you. If she does nothing, then that is what you will record, what does she do instead? If she plays, how does she play, what does she play with, what does she do exactly?

RELAXATION [IN CRATE, BED, FAVORITE ROOM WITH DOG MUSIC or classical, soft, sleepy music]

NEXT ONE FULL HOUR OF RELAXATION. (This should take you close to lunchtime.)

What does relaxation look like? It looks like this:

- body tone is lucid,
- dog is fully relaxed,
- eyes closed,
- head on paws or to side,
- relaxed to side of hip or flat body,
- shoulders soft –
- total and ultimate relaxation also may have a SIGH, a DEEP SIGH or more attached to it, as the dog releases emotional stress to feel relaxed.

OBSERVE

What happens during this time? Record sighs, yawns, any calming signals you see.

This is important. Video and/or digital photos during any of the above or below or pieces is appropriate.

ALONE TIME

Just before lunch and after second RELAXATION period, let dog just wander around the house. You play invisible dog – do not talk to her nor acknowledge she is there (no matter what she does at this point). Get involved in something, paying bills etc. but keep an eye on her to see how she is handling this.

Answer these questions:

- What does she do?
- How does she entertain herself?
- Does she bark? Pace? Or does she settle down? Look for toys? Stick by you? What?

HALFWAY THROUGH YOUR DAY – It should be lunchtime.

LUNCHTIME FOR YOU

Make lunch special for you and continue playing invisible dog until you are done.

Afterwards prepare for activity #1. When you play invisible dog, it makes your words more worth listening to, your cues more valuable, your time spent even more bonding and relationship building. You are asking dog to "give you a break" – a game played by Leslie McDevitt in her book "Control Unleashed" or simply "playing hard to get".

MENTALLY STIMULATING GAME #1. Color Recognition.

SET-UP: One on one with Chai.

Little colored plastic easter eggs work well OR four to six different colored objects all dog's size, so small, medium or large. You want to set her up for success.

Put dog on a sit/stay 5 feet away.

Place colored object five feet in front of her. Start with yellow OR blue. Just one object. This is the object that will always have food under it.

Ask her to find 20 times. Yes, reset it from 1 to 3 above. Same color. This is so she can create a memory of the color that has the food. When we add more colors, she will then go straight to the yellow or blue no matter what.

Can dogs distinguish colors? Yes, they can. They have rods and cones in their eyes like we do, however, they may distinguish color more as lighter tones, grays, blacks. They cannot see reds. Green looks white for instance. They see more grays in their line of sight. Yellows and blues are very distinguishable (in a lighter tone than we see them – but nonetheless – color).

NEXT: ADD a second color (may be as far as you go, that is okay. Do 20 trials and write down how often she gets it right, even when you switch the position (right, left so 10 each). Does dog go right for the proper color. This will show us a lot about how she learns, processes information, and distinguishes color, and even smell.

NEXT: Add a third color. 20 repetitions. NEXT: a fourth. AND you can do a fifth and sixth if you like.

TESTING: This is what you are looking for...

- Does dog distinguish color.
- Is she sensitive to color?
- Do the objects scare her?
- QUESTIONS TO CONSIDER
- What egg or colored cup does she go to.
- How does she approach the task – does she think about it?

Or move in too quickly making wrong decisions to find the food and not really looking at the color?

- Does she walk away?
- Does she need more encouragement?
- OR does she really enjoy participation?

Any and all observations please, as it effects how dog "thinks" and the process of behavior modification and even skill work. It also has a lot to say about her personality.

TOY PLAY AGAIN, Interactive

Just like in the morning – EXCEPT YOU **WILL INTERACT** WITH DOG – a 15-minute interactive play period with you. **Observe and report.**

Pile toys again from box. Better to do this one on one.

Tease a little by putting a toy behind your back, then give it to her. Throw a toy. Say it's yours and she cannot have it. Squiggle it on the floor to entice play. I know she loves this activity – so do inside or out.

Play a find it game by hiding bits of chicken under or in toys and say, "find it!". What does she do? You can encourage. Even pretend to find it yourself and pretend to eat the chicken.

What you want to see is dog start to develop interest, becomes involved, and even starts to have interest in certain toys.

When the buzzer goes off. Throw up your hands and say, "That'll do" (or whatever cue you use). And pick up all the toys, put them back into the box EXCEPT FOR TWO TOYS she showed interest in. Leave those out and put the rest up high or with a lid on them.

RELAXATION

1 hour relaxation period with intent for deep sleep. This allows dog to process all the positive information, the mental activity and to really start to de-stress.

Full relaxation (at this time of day) may be a foreign concept. She may respond by going through a slight extinction burst (meaning reactivity might occur) OR she may just be visibly calmer, fall asleep faster etc. Let her sleep, that is important. If after an hour she is still asleep, do not wake her, just let her wake naturally.

THUNDERSHIRT OR WRAP:

AFTER DOG AWAKENS WRAP – ½ wrap. …..according to the diagram. The wrap is very calming and puts the dog into an understanding of body connections. It relaxes tight muscles. Once the wrap is on…simply walk dog around the room and then take it off.

IF YOU USE the Thundershirt. Record.

MENTALLY STIMULATING ACTIVITY #2

Size recognition. Can dog distinguish size? How does she handle changes in size? Important in evaluating how she relates to the environment and changes.

SET UP – SIZE:

- Containers neutral color and start with two. I would use the small size first.
- (Do a few warm-ups with one – the small container – about 10).
- Then add a second container, a different size.

- The reward will always be under the small container, no matter how many (at this stage) containers or in what location it ends up.
- THEN add a third.

WHAT DO YOU OBSERVE DOG DOING? Do 10 repetitions each. WRITE out your observations.

DINNER TIME

OFFER up one meat source 1 cup or if you felt breakfast was a bit insufficient or over-sufficient based on what dog is telling you.

EVENING: How the day ends is as important as how it starts. You want dog to process positive things, zero reactivity so she sleeps peacefully and deeply and is refreshed for the next day. The toxins have now started to release.

Play period **outdoors**. The goal is that dog sleeps a full 8 HOURS…no exception. SO, make sure that once she goes to bed that comfort is key. Let me know if she had 8 hours, if not, by the end of the detox this should be naturally occurring.

End day with relaxation time before bedtime. Possibly a Kong filled with detox acceptable food – to work her mouth OR a marrow bone.

SEND YOUR REPORT TO ME by 6 PM your time. (I am interested in her snarling/growling and anti-social behaviors toward, you, strangers, and the cats. There is ALWAYS a reason -)

Send client day two and comments on DAY ONE and your OBSERVATIONS.

DAY TWO and DAY THREE are then **customized** based on the CED Cycle (Chapter five) and on what was observed in DAY ONE.

Appendix 6

CED FAQ SHEET – Commonly asked questions

Below are in alphabetical order based on categories

ALONE TIME – i play invisible dog)

QUESTION: Can the other animals be around too during these periods? or best not?

ANSWER: It shouldn't matter if the others are around, IF they don't cause stress – i.e. over-barking where everyone joins in etc.

QUESTION: What is the difference between "relaxation time" and "alone time".

ANSWER: The alone time exercise can cross over into a relaxation period for some dogs or a into noninteractive toy play. It depends on the dog. There might be no difference, either way, no big deal. The purpose of relaxation period is to set the stage for deep REM sleep. That means music, touch, a safe zone where it means sleep. Alone time just allows dog to do what they want, not necessarily in a safe zone, and no pre-setup. It is to see if the dog can self-soothe, or do they attention seek, do they follow you around, do they bark, what? Don't over think it and remember there is no right or wrong. It is just do it and observe.

COLD – sensory exercise

QUESTION: How long should I lay the pack of ice on each spot? A moment?

ANSWER: A moment. Some dogs love the ice, others not so much. This is just a sensory test.

COLOR RECOGNITION

QUESTION: Eggs: Should I put a 1/2 egg down with food under it, or put a whole egg down with food inside it, or a whole egg down with food behind it? (It says put an object down with food under it)

ANSWER: 1/2 egg (whole egg would be more advanced). Food should be under it. An advanced portion of this is that the dog "touch the yellow with his nose" (a target game actually) and you click and reward this, but some need encouragement and smell and color help them to be successful. See what your dog does.

QUESTION: I put yellow down for 20 trials. I say "find yellow", he does, and his reward is immediate (the food) so I don't need to mark it?

ANSWER: Not unless you are doing the target the yellow exercise, with no food undereath. I use the clicker very little in the CED as it "activates" the dog. I want to "de-activate them", tire their brain. Some dogs are advanced enough in skills and clicker training to be able to do this exercise as a target/touch exercise. In that case, no food is under the yellow egg, but touching the yellow is the only one that gets marked and rewarded.

QUESTION: 20 trials later, I add the blue next to the yellow. I say "find blue". He goes for yellow... but – where is the food in this second set of 20 trials?

ANSWER: It is always one color choice dog is to find (yellow or blue, not both). Only the color chosen has any food under it or associated with it throughout the exercise.

QUESTION: Am I only asking him to "find blue" and placing the food under the blue?

ANSWER: Again, you are just adding a color, if you've chosen yellow, then reward is always under the color yellow. That is why the process of committing yellow to memory. Yellow equals food (other color equals no food, ever).

QUESTION: Am I alternating randomly between yellow and blue? If I am alternating, does he need to go out of the room in between trials so I can set the food down underneath the appropriate color without him seeing this?

ANSWER: No, not alternating, just color yellow (or blue, if you chose this – blue and yellow are what a dog can see more clearly then other colors). Sending dog out of room could be an advanced portion of this activity. Most dogs are NOT this advanced in CED. If he is super good with this, you can do an advanced version later or change the activity instructions to indicate a more advanced exercise. The point is an eye test of sorts, to see if the dog can see yellow or blue.

QUESTION: Or am I putting the food under the yellow and telling him to find blue and then marking when he approaches blue and treating from my hidden stash?

ANSWER: Gosh too confusing! Keep it simple and put food under yellow only, no matter how many colors you put down the dog always finds the food under yellow and no matter where the yellow is in the mix of other colors. Here is a video of Standard Poodle, Zoe, doing the color game at a more advanced click/treat stage: https://www.youtube.com/watch?v=lwrVEwpnJEw

Over-analyzing or being a perfectionist.

For those who over-analyze or are perfectionists, I always say there is no right or wrong to the CED – it is observation and so relax, so it can be fun, stress free and progressive. Each dog will respond differently to activities, touch dependent on where they are in their stress, their learning, their stage of life.

DETOX DIET

QUESTION: How do you assess "is he still hungry afterwards"? He's a typical dog — he always wants to eat !!

ANSWER: Does he look satisfied, walks away from the bowl or acts like he wants more to eat. Does he lick the bowl, ask for more food, or does he walk away, go lie down, looks satisfied? In the detox we want them to eat to satiation.

QUESTION: After breakfast: does he need to be "still" to relax? Or can we just go about our day and he will lay on the couch and be calm on his own as per the usual?

ANSWER: Just to relax. Do no ask him to lie down, or force relaxation in any way. It has to come naturally from the dog so your job is to provide the cozy atmosphere where that can take place, i.e. music, a cozy bed. The dog may or may not relax these first few times. Again, no right or wrong. To come down from stress takes time and observing exactly what he does do, and following the steps in the order written are key.

QUESTION: Do I need to have Halibut on me all day to be prepared for the trucks that drive by?

ANSWER: Sure, why not? Or other rewards she can "have" . You are making trucks a good emotional experience. You can also have toy play she loves. It has to be a reward she loves above all else as you are dealing with a HIGH distraction. And yes, continuous reinforcement until you see signs that a) she hears and looks at truck b) decides to look at you instead c) JACKPOT.

GAMES

QUESTION: For take it/give it game, my dog doesn't like to take things. The only thing she sometimes takes is a bully stick and she takes them and walks away (to either hide or chew in private). Should I just shape then when she looks at the toy and when she puts her nose/mouth on the toy.

ANSWER: Yes shape it – no pressure – just get what you can and have fun doing it. I want to see what she does, how she thinks – not thinking is also something. It would be a fun exercise and "assume nothing".

OTHER DOGS IN HOUSEHOLD

QUESTION: I will need to give them some activity, when is best? A good run in the morning and an activity at night and they will be restful most of the day. Is there a time when I can leave my dog to sleep and take other dogs into the garage for some training or out for a walk?

ANSWER: Answering this question with a question. Can dog doing CED relax and destress if the dogs go out for a walk? training? If not, then it will be stressful, not stress releasing. So base decisions on this. I have had a few families do really well with their CED dog and the other dogs in the household all just seem to relax together. I would rather during relaxation times that all relax. Mental activities, games for the other dogs might be key element and they will be curious as to what dog going through CEDj is doing. The goal is always deep uninterrupted sleep to achieve nREM – REM – nREM where healing and energy enhancement occurs, the good neurotransmitters activate.

QUESTION: Does dog need to be kept segregated from the other dogs or is it okay to mingle when taking her out to toilet etc. Getting her from one place to another will involve the other dogs who all get on and will be fine other than wondering why she is being special. If she wants to do a zoomy around the garden or play in between, is this okay, or are we moving from one area to another with as little distraction as possible?

ANSWER: Again segregation for some dogs can be stressful, others it is destressing. Usually going outdoors or potty and mingling is really good for the dog(s). Should be fine. let the treats flow to get saliva flowing in between times so it is fun and relaxing for all. If she is doing zoomies she is in fool around behavior and that is high stress, but it will be information for us and yes it is ok if it is a play sequence, but not a stress sequence. If dog is just running around but not crazed by zoomies for instance. It isn't the distraction itself that is worrisome, but if the distraction is stress increasing versus stress releasing. For instance exercise can create stress versus release it and so then it is not very beneficial. Each has to make a realistic call or judgement on this.

OUTDOORS: (awareness walk or regular daily walkks)

QUESTION: It is nearly impossible to go on a nice walk and to avoid dogs (especially city dogs). While he doesn't have a huge reaction, there is still an element of stress here. Should I keep outside time to just potty breaks? OR should I have another play session with him of some sort at night instead?

ANSWER: If a dog is highly reactive (or chances of seeing triggers are 100%) then yes, just potty breaks. You can do walks indoors and obstacle work as physical stimulation. If a walk is stressful it builds glucocorticoids, instead of reducing them, so no walks. The dog can have a chew to tire and exercise his mouth muscles. too, as another alternative.

QUESTION: OUTDOORS PART 2: Should the dog's regular walks be taken during the detox, if they are not reactive to dogs or people? If it is their favorite thing to do?

ANSWER: It depends. Normally, no not during a CED. There are exceptions and need to be evaluated by trainer working the case. An awareness walk, in a quiet area, like a cemetary might be doable. This walk is usually no longer than ten to 20 minutes and just to get dog moving and outside.

PLAY, first five minutes:

When I put stuff down, I can almost guarantee that my dog will pick up a toy and bring it to me for a game of tug. Should I not interact with him?

ANSWER: You must just be passive with him during this period of non-interactive to play. We are observing how creative he is, can he self-soothe, does he enjoy playing on his own. If not, that is an observation as well. It will be harder for you than him. Just let him do what he wants during this time. There will be an interactive toy period later in the CED.

REACTIVITY

QUESTION. Can you clarify 'no reactions'? Is this any excitement or just 'reactivity'. I.e., she will get excited over hearing the cat door, or letting her out the back sometimes charges at the chickens or hearing a jingling collar down the street.

ANSWER: Meaning distress caused by the environment that increases barking, or other stress behaviors. No charging anything should be key and definitely no charging the chickens. Take dog out on lead to prevent that. Desensitization to jingling collars should occur by feeding through the noise. Identify what excitement over the cat door looks like? Go to YouTube or Google and see if you can locate some jingling collar sounds.

RELAXATION periods:

QUESTION: Should I just let him chill on couch/bed as he normally would? Make sure he has some comfy blankets, etc to curl up on?

ANSWER: Yes, just set the stage, distraction free as possible – music or TV to drown out distractive sounds, and you'll be doing warm towels – from the dryer as your first relax period exercise, that usually sets the tone. If you have relaxing things you can use, or a favorite cuddle toy Grayson likes – it is your goal to set him up for success just as you would in a training session. Except this time it is for a successful relaxation period. He might not relax at all this period – that is ok, again there is no right or wrong.

QUESTION: My dog has total relaxation, with sighs and all, when he is cuddled up with mommy and daddy in bed. Or if he is in his crate, with the door open, and tired at the end of the day. Not sure how to set him up for him being so relaxed that he "sighs" during the day! Should I encourage him onto the bed and set him up to cuddle with me relaxed? Or let him decide where he wants to curl up?

ANSWER: I would say just don't worry about it. You can lie down with him, that is ok. The goal is that he sleeps so deeply he would not know if you moved and went away, that probably won't come until later in the process. If he doesn't achieve this, it is pretty obvious he is acutely or chronically stressed for whatever reason we may not understand. If that occurs, a second 3 day CED is a part of the process, one month later OR if you can do it, more days in a row nowt. You will learn a lot about your dog during this process. Dogs need to sleep 12 to 14 hours a day, two to four of those hours during the day.

QUESTION: Afternoon relaxation: is the goal one hour of sleep?

ANSWER: The goal is deep sleep – one hour or more or 20M , whatever the dog is ready for at that time. It is a process, so let it happen. You cannot force a dog to sleep anymore than you can force yourself to sleep. Set the stage, keep it quiet for an hour, see what the dog can manage to do. It is like asking, is the goal in just learning the teeter to do the teeter in agility in one day? Probably not, you have to work up to it. So just let it happen. Time it to one hour, see how your dog does. The process is the dog will rest, relax, calm (in this phase they might fight sleep, or won't be able to let their guard down) in order to get to nonREM, REM and then back out into nonREM. In REM you'll see rapid eye movement at least, maybe some twitching. nonREM dog will appear very groggy and want to lie down, ease out of sleep. So when the word "sleep" is said or written, it assumes REM. A dog's REM is about nine minutes long, shorter than a human REM, and why a dog needs more sleep. The dog might go in and out of REM up to four times a night. On the flip side, if dog is sleeping deeply, do not wake them up, let them awaken naturally.

QUESTION: When my dog is resting I note that I can be with her, but can I also leave her or is it preferable that I am near? Can my other dog(s) also be near if she is quiet and also resting?

ANSWER: We are working toward sleep so deep that when you get up, your dog does not hear you, or get up. Tt is when the ultimate goal for the CED. You can leave your dog, but it depends on the dog. Yes, she can be near you. There have been many two dog detoxes, dog actually does CED and the other benefits from the dog destressing and the relaxation periods themselves. Your call, but all calls need to be made on the question of, is this stressing or destressing your dog?

QUESTION: How will I know she is fully relaxed?

ANSWER: By her body muscle tone. It will look like she's sinking into it, soft, no worries and more. Her head will seem too heavy to hold, she might fight full relaxation but her eyes will be too heavy too keep open. You want to see a puddle of fur.

RESPIRATION EVALUATION:

QUESTION: Can I do this before we go outside (and he is active/excited) or should I do this in order listed – potty then evaluate respiration?

ANSWER: If he gets excited for his potty, then take his resting respiration before you go out. Reverse the order. That is a-ok and I can tell you know your dog pretty well!

SIZE RECOGNITION QUESTIONS:

- Are containers different sizes but same color?
- Should they be opaque?
- Is the treat underneath?
- Do I cue "find it" or smilar? Or just put the container there and wait for them to touch it nose/paw and then reward?

ANSWER: Yes, containers are different sizes, with intent that the reward is easily distinguishable by the dog, either small size, or large size. It is more important they are different sizes than opaque or not. Yes you can cue find it, treat is under the size you are working with only, AND if t dog is more advanced – you can just have them touch (w/o food under) and reward the right size. Most dogs are NOT that advanced. With food under, they CAN tip it over and get the reward.

QUESTION: is it important that **they not see the treat underneath**?

ANSWER: Not important that they see the treat (they'll smell it too) . Dogs see differently then we do so it might blend in.

QUESTION: Is there a video of this activity in action?

ANSWER:

https://www.youtube.com/watch?v=Zyx2UKJ9Jv4 within step-by-step directions there is a photo of it and it should be very clear 1, 2, 3. You start with 10 to 20 repetitions of just memory of small or large container. Then add a second (usually the tallest or the smallest – so there is a big difference in size). 10 or 20 repetitions (going for 80% success) – then add a third size.

QUESTION: Am I just putting food under a small container for 20 trials, then adding another container for 20 trials, but still keeping the food under the small container, and then adding a third container for 20 trials, but still keeping the food under the small container... just to see what he's going to do? This is more an observational exercise than a training exercise?

AMSWER: SMALL ONLY always has food under it. No other. (NOTE: that said if you use large size, be consistent. Then the large will have food under it, ONLY.) The 20 trials are so the dog commits the size that contains the reward to memory . Tells how they learn. It is a mentally tiring exercise where dog has to think. Yes, it is different from toy play, training exercises etc. LET THE DOG THINK it through. Al the exercises throughout the CED are observational whereby information is gathered about the individual.

TTOUCH – wraps

QUESTION: We only have 2-inch ace bandages here, I got that and hope its ok

ANSWER: That's ok too – just either fold in half – or cut them into 1″.

QUESTION: When working on TTouch and lifting her legs, what happens if she is on one side? How do I access the other side without flipping her

ANSWER: You don't need to work the other side. The body will feel what you've done on one side and process it for the other side. Cells are amazing things. Also make sure your thumb is flat on her body, no poking. Breath, relax into it for yourself, and make small circle that move the skin at a pressure comfortable to dog. If you hold your breath, so will she. No flipping and if she wants to move away, let her, she'll come back,and then you continue.

TREATS

QUESTION: If she runs away do I follow her with the food and try to get her to take it?

ANSWER: NOPE no following with food. You walk in the opposite direction. If she runs away a) the duration of the exercise was too long b) the distance too short or c) the distraction too intense. Do not put dog in the path of a distraction (that is flooding, too much information at a distance they cannot handle) to get her to hear it or see it,. Just work with her through it as it occurs in real life at proper distance. You can drop the treat, but make sure she sees it and loves it. This will lower her head, which releases tension . You can't be relaxed and reactive at the same time. Also you can tell her it is ok, as you feed her the food.

QUESTION: Should breakfast be smaller because I am stuffing a huge Kong for her for later in the day? Should I portion half of breakfast and half of dinner into the kong?

ANSWER: Yes.

WARMTH – sensory exercise

QUESTION: When it says Ttouch and a 1/2 wrap", am I "doing" Ttouch? Should I be doing a particular type of ttouch technique on a certain body part/for a specific length of time?

ANSWER: Yes, there should be an element of physical touch. Here is a video to emulate and don't worry if you don't know Ttouch. Do what the video displays, as much or as little as you want. The goal is that the dog enjoys it. He can move away any time he wants to, no force to stay. If he returns, continue. End in moments if he hasn't done this before, and if you see any stress signals, just end. Let dog guide you. Let the dog to choose to be touched etc. So use CC & DS with the anxiety coat and/or wraps too. Here is the video: https://www.youtube.com/watch?v=84tW1XjuKnk Other videos can be seen at www.tellington-touch.com.

Resources

Articles

Bekoff, Marc, Ph.D. Animal Emotions, Aggression in Dogs: The Roles of Oxytocin and Vasopressin; A new study shows these hormones can shape both affiliation and aggression, Oct 05, 2017, Psychology Today *(Book: Chapter 3)* https://www.psychologytoday.com/blog/animal-emotions/201710/aggression-in-dogs-the-roles-oxytocin-and-vasopressin *(Book: Chapter 7)*

Bekoff, Marc 1995 Social Play Behaviour Cooperation, Fairness, Trust, and the Evolution of Morality *(Book: Chapter 16)*

Frediani, Jodi *Certified TTOUCH Companion Animal Instructor and TTEAM Horse Practitioner: Trying to Ease Your Dog's Stress, article published in Whole Dog Journal January 2000 (Book: Chapter 1)* http://www.whole-dog-journal.com/issues/3_1/features/Easing-Your-Dogs-Stress_5031-1.html

The Primary Headship newsletter, April 2007 *(Book: Chapter 2, 3)*

Blogs

Garrod, Diane, Canine Seizures (Chancellor's real-life journey) https://dgarrod.wordpress.com/

Garrod, Diane, Can you fix my dog, Pet Professional's Guild (PPG) blog http://ppgworldservices.com/2015/05/08/can-you-fix-my-dog/

Hanson, Don, Green Acres Kennel Shop blog "Understanding, Identifying and Coping with Canine Stress" *(Book: Chapter 2, 3)*

PPG Blogs by the Guild, 10 Ways to use problem-solving games in behavior modification, by Diane Garrod http://ppgworldservices.com/2014/11/18/ten-ways-to-use-problem-solving-games-in-behavior-modification/ *(Book: Chapter 8)*

PPG Blogs by the Guild, Ongoing study with street dogs shows what they do on a day-to-day basis. A PPG blog on Lives of Streeties – A Study on Free Ranging Dogs http://ppgworldservices.com/2016/01/20/lives-of-streeties-a-study-on-free-ranging-dogs/ says, EXCERPT: *"But even with 400 videos, patterns emerged. The first big takeaway for me was that these street dogs love one activity more than any other. In fact, it's just one activity that occupies 40 per cent of their activity profile. And there are close to 15 different activities that I identified they are engaged in. But just one takes the biggest amount of their time – sleeping. Dogs love to snooze." (Book-Chapter 10)*

Books

Alexander, Melissa, Click for Joy http://www.clickersolutions.com/reviews/clickforjoy.htm

Arrowsmith, Claire, Brain Games *(Book: Chapter 8)*

Berns, Gregory, Neuroeconomics Professor essay, *New York Times* "Dogs Are People, Too" ; book *"How Dogs Love Us: A Neuroscientist and His Adopted Dog Decode the Canine Brain"* *(New Harvest, 2013) (Book: Chapter 7)*

Birmelin, Immanuel How Dogs Think: A Guide to Beautiful Relationships, 2006, Chapter 1 *(Book: Chapter 6, 8)*

Birmelin, Immanuel, Biologist, How Dogs Think, A Guide to a Beautiful Relationship pp. 68/69; 72/73; 80 to 87; *(Book: Chapter 10)*

Bradshaw, John, Dog Sense, 148 -181 (6) 2011 *(Book: Chapter 5, 6)*

Brown, Ali, M.Ed., CPDT, "Scaredy Dog!" 2004: Stress Puppy 15(1); 18 (1) *(Book: Chapter 1)*

Coppinger & Coppinger (2001) Dogs: A Startling New Understanding of Canine Origin, Behavior & Evolution *(Book: Chapter 15)*

Kis Anna, Sára Szakadát, Márta Gácsi, Enikő Kovács, Péter Simor, Csenge Török, Ferenc Gombos, Róbert Bódizs, József Topáll, (2017). The interrelated effect of sleep and learning in dogs (Canis familiaris), an EEG and behavioral study. Scientific Reports, 7, 41873, doi: 10.1038/srep41873 https://www.researchgate.net/publication/313401175_The_interrelated_effect_of_sleep_and_learning_in_dogs_Canis_familiaris_An_EEG_and_behavioural_study *(Book: Chapter 10)*

LeDoux, J. (1996) The Emotional Brain, Simon and Schuster Inc., New York *(Book: Chapter 6)*

O'Heare, James: Aggressive Behavior in Dogs, 2007; 109 (5) *(Book: Chapter 2, 3)*

O'Heare, James: Canine Neuropsychology, 2005, 3rd edition *(Book: Chapter 2, 3)*

Olmert, Meg Daly: Made for each other, studies oxytocin *(Book-Chapter 11, 15)*

Panksepp, J. (2005b) Affective consciousness: Core emotions in animals and humans. Consciousness and Cognition *(Book: Chapter 6)*

Pert, Candace, Neuroscientist: Molecules of Emotion, The Science Behind the Mind 1997, 1999 *(Book: Chapter 1)*

Sapolsky, Robert, Stanford University neuroscientist: Why Zebras Do not Get Ulcers 1994, 1998 *(Book: Chapter 1, 7)*

Scholz, Martina and von Reinhardt, Clarissa, Stress in Dogs, 2007 *(Book: Chapter 2)*

Shettleworth, Sara 1998 Cognition, Evolution and Behaviour *(Book: Chapter 16)*

Simonov, Pavel Vasil'evich, The Motivated Brain: A Neurophysiological Analysis of Human Behavior *(Book: Chapter 6)*

Strong, Val: The Dog's Brain – A Simple Guide, 1999 *(Book: Chapter 2, 3)*

Tellington, Linda, Getting in Ttouch with your dog *(Book: Chapter 2)* http://www.ttouch.com/shop/index.php?productID=171

Uvnas-Moberg, Dr. Kerstin, The Oxytocin Factor *(Book: Chapter 11, 15)*

Cited works and other sources

Note: sources are cited throughout the book, not necessarily recommendations. See text for more information. They are listed in alphabetical order and the chapter the reference is located in this book is listed in parenthesis.

Beery, AK and **Francis, DD**. Adaptive significance of natural variations in maternal care in rats: a translational perspective. *Neuroscience and Biobehavioral Reviews* 2011 35(7): 1552-1561 *(Book: Chapter 7)*

Beery, AK, Lacey, EA and **Francis, DD** (2008). Oxytocin and Vasopressin Receptor Distributions in a Solitary and a Social Species of Tuco-Tuco (Ctenomys haigi and Ctenomys sociabilis) *Journal of Comparative Neurology*507:1847-1859 *(Book: Chapter 7)*

Bekoff, Marc "Scans Reveal Striking Similarity Between Human and Canine Minds (Op-Ed)", October 18, 2013 *Animal Emotions in Psychology Today. Article attributed to LiveScience's* Expert Voices: Op-Ed & Insights.

Belanoff JK, Gross K, Yager A, Schatzberg AF (2001). "Corticosteroids and cognition". J Psychiatr Res 35 (3): 127–45. doi:10.1016/S0022-3956(01)00018-8. PMID 11461709. *(Book: Chapter 1)*

Bowen, R. May 2006, Colorado State, "Glucocorticoids" *(Book: Chapter 1)*

Bradshaw, John *Dog Sense* citation number 13, page 300 and CH 5 in Bradshaw's book, page 145 Subsequent research has shown that dogs' stress hormone levels are different depending not only on the gender of their pet guardians or careers (lower if they are women) but also on their personalities (lower if the pet guardians are extroverts).

Cahill L, McGaugh JL (July 1998). "Mechanisms of emotional arousal and lasting declarative memory". Trends Neurosci. 21 (7): 294–9. PMID 9683321. *(Book: Chapter 1)*

Cajori, F.A., "The Enzyme Activity of Dog's Intestinal Juice and It's Relation to Intestinal Digestion", Department of Physiological Chemistry,

School of Medicine, University of Pennsylvania, Pittsburg; March 16, 1933. *(See Book Chapter 6)*

Carlson, N.R. (2010). Physiology of Behavior, 11th Edition. New York: Allyn & Bacon. p. 605. *(Book: Chapter 1)*

Divorsky, George "Brain scans show dogs are as conscious as human children", October 2013 Neuroscience AND "Prominent scientists sign declaration that animals have conscious awareness, just like us" August 2012 Cambridge Declaration on Consciousness(Book: Chapter 7)Eisenberger, NI and Lieberman MD, 2004 Why rejection hurts: a common neural alarm system for physical and social pain – Trends in cognitive sciences (Book: Chapter 10)

Francis, DD (2009). Conceptualizing Child Health Disparities: A Role for Developmental Neurogenomics. *Pediatrics* 124 Suppl 3: S196-202 *(Book: Chapter 7)*

Francis, D.D, Szegda, K., Campbell, G., Martin, W.D. and Insel, T.R. (2003). Epigenetic sources of behavioral differences in mice. *Nature Neuroscience.* 6 (5): 445-446. *(Book: Chapter 7)*

Francis, D.D., Diorio, J., Plotsky, P.M. and Meaney, M.J. (2002). Environmental Enrichment reverses the effects of maternal separation on stress reactivity. *(Book: Chapter 7)*

Francis, D.D. Young, L.J., Meaney, M.J. and Insel, T.R. (2002). Naturally occurring differences in material care are associated with the expression of oxytocin and vasopressin (V1a) receptors: gender differences. *Journal of Neuroendocrinology.* 14(14):349-353. *(Book: Chapter 7)*

Francis,D.D. Champagne, F.C., and Meaney, M.J. (2000). Individual differences in maternal behavior are associated with variations in oxytocin receptor levels in rat. *Journal of Neuroendocrinology.* 12(12): 1145-1148. *(Book: Chapter 7)*

Francis, D.D. Caldji, C., Champagne, F., Plotsky, P.M. and Meaney, M.J. (1999). The Role of corticotrophin-releasing factor <ETH> norepinephrine systems in mediating the effects of early experience on the development of behavioral and endocrine Responses to stress. *Biological Psychiatry.* 46(9):1153-1166. *(Book: Chapter 7)*

Francis D.D., Diorio, J., Liu, D. and Meaney, M.J. (1999). Variations in maternal care Form the basis for a non-genomic mechanism of inter-generational transmission of individual differences in behavioral and endocrine responses to stress. *Science.* 286(5442):1155-8. *(Book: Chapter 7)*

Francis, D.D. and Meaney, M.J. (1999). Maternal care and the development of stress responses. *Curr Opin Neurobiol.* 9, 128-134. *(Book: Chapter 7)*

Franklin, Zijlstra & Muris, 2006; Are nonpharmacological induced rewards related to anhedonia? A study among skydivers. Progress in Neuro-Psychopharmacology & Biological Psychiatry, 30, 297-300 *(Book: Chapter 10, 15)*

Hess, U., & Thibault, P. (2009). Darwin and emotion expression. American Psychological Association, 64(2), 120-128. doi: American Psychologist. *(Book: Chapter 6)*

Jensen, K, Hahn, N, Palme, R and **Francis, DD** (in press). Vacuum cleaner noise and acute stress responses in female C57BL/6 mice (Mus musculus). *Journal of the American Association for Laboratory Animal Science (Book: Chapter 7)*

LeDoux, Jospeh, The Emotional Brain: The Mysterious Underpinnings of Emotional Life (New York: Touchstone Books), 1996 *(Book: Chapter 10)*

LeDoux, Joseph E., Synaptic Self: How Our Brains Become Who We are, 2003 *(Book: Chapter 10)*

Lewin, Jo and Torrens, Kerry, Royal Society of Medicine, the Complementary and Natural Healthcare Council (CNHC), and the British Association for Applied Nutrition and Nutritional Therapy (BANT) *(Book: Chapter 11)*

Liu,D., Diorio, J., Day, J.C., **Francis, D.D.** and Meaney, M.J. (2000). Maternal care, hippocampal synaptogenesis, and cognitive development in rats. *Nature Neuroscience.* 3(8): 799-806. *(Book: Chapter 7)*

Lui, D., Diorio, J., Tannenbaum, B., Caldji, C., **Francis D.D.**, Freedman. A., Sharma, S., Pearson, D., Plotsky, P.M., and Meaney, M.J. (1997) Maternal care, hippocampal glucocorticoid receptors, and hypothalamic-pituitary-adrenal responses to stress. *Science.* 277,1659-1662. *(Book: Chapter 7)*

Lupien SJ, Maheu F, Tu M, Fiocco A, Schramek TE (2007). "The effects of stress and stress hormones on human cognition: Implications for the field of brain and cognition". Brain and Cognition 65: 209–237. doi: 10.1016/j.bandc.2007.02.007. PMID 17466428. *(Book: Chapter 1)*

McMillan & Rollin, 2001, Greenspan & Baars, 2005, Lecas, 2006 *(Book: Chapter 6)*

Meaney, M.J., Diorio, J., **Francis, D.D.**, Weaver., S., Yau, J., Chapman, K. and Seckl, J.R. (2000). Poistnatal Handling increases the expression pf cAMP-inducible Transcription factors in the rat hippocampus: The Environmental enrichment reverses the Effects of maternal separation on stress reactivity effects of thyroid hormones and serotonin. *Journal of Neuroscience.* 20(10): 3926-3935. *(Book: Chapter 7)*

Panksepp, Jaak (2005, 2006), the FEAR SYSTEM manifests in the mid-brain – and stays there – MANIFESTS fear whether there is or is not something to fear – perceived fear – i.e., thunderstorms. This is where long-standing fears stay and are hardest to rehabilitate. *(Book: Chapter 2)*

Panksepp, Jaak "Affective neuroscience: the foundations of human and animal emotions" Oxford University Press, 2004, ISBN: 019517805X) is the definitive summary of the evidence for the seven core emotional systems discussed *(Book: Chapter 6)*

Panksepp, Jaak 2005a, 2005b Affective consciousness: Core emotional feelings in animals and humans *(Book: Chapter 10)*

Panksepp, Jaak in Affective Neuroscience: The Foundations of Human and Animal Emotions, *1998 (Book: Chapter 10)*

Panksepp, Jaak in The Involvement of Nucleus Accumbens Dopamine in Appetitive and Aversive Motivation, 1994 *(Book: Chapter 10)*

Panksepp, Jaak, PhD, in Affective neuroscience of the emotional Brain Mind: evolutionary perspectives and implications for understanding depression, Dialogues Clinical Neuroscience. 2010 Dec; 12(4): 533–545 *(Book: Chapter 10)*

Phillipson, E.A., Murphy, E. , Kozar, L.F., Regulation of respiration in sleeping dogs. Journal of Applied Physiology Published 1 May 1976 **Vol.** 40 **no.** 688-693 *(Book: Chapter 12)*

Rosado, Belen, Blood concentrations of serotonin, cortisol and dehydroepiandrosterone in aggressive dogs. Applied Animal Behaviour Science (Impact Factor: 1.63). 03/2010; 123:124-130. DOI: 10.1016/j. applanim.2010.01.009 *(Book: Chapter 15)*

Sakhai, SA, Kriegsfeld, LJ and **Francis, DD.** The Impact of Early Life and Parental Care on the Sexual Development of Long-Evans Rats. *Psychoneuroendocrinology.* 2011 *(Book: Chapter 7)*

Sapolsky RM (October 1994). "Glucocorticoids, stress and exacerbation of excitotoxic neuron death". Seminars in Neuroscience 6 (5): 323–331. doi:10.1006/smns.1994.1041. *(Book: Chapter 1)*

Sapolsky, Robert M., Stress and Plasticity in the Limbic, Neurochemical research, Vol. 28, No. 11, 2003 pp. 1735 – 1742. *(Book: Chapter 7)*

Saxton, K, John-Henderson, N, Reid, MW and **Francis, DD.** The social environment and iIL-6 in rats and humans. *Brain, Behavior, and Immunity* 2011 *(Book: Chapter 7)*

Scholz, Martina and von Reinhardt, Clarissa, Stress in Dogs, 2007 *(Book: Chapter 3)*

Segal, Daniel J. MD, and Bryson, Tina Payne in Time magazine, "Time Outs" Are Hurting Your Child, September 23, 2013 *(Book: Chapter 10)*

Siegel, Daniel J. MD, The Developing Mind, Second Edition: How Relationships and the Brain Interact to Shape Who We Are, February 27, 2012 *(Book: Chapter 10)*

Simonov, Pavel Vasil'evich, The Motivated Brain: A Neurophysiological Analysis of Human Behavior pg. 35 *(Book: Chapter 6)*

Simonov PV, Neurosci Behav Physiol. 1990 May-Jun;20(3):230-5. "Reflexes of purpose and freedom" in the comparative physiology of higher nervous activity. *(Book: Chapter 6)*

Suchodolski,, Jan S., Texas A & M University, Veterinary medicine and biomedical sciences, med. vet., Dr. med. vet. PhD, DACVM "*We are just beginning to understand how this microbiota interacts with the host and thereby exhibiting an influence that reaches beyond the gastrointestinal tract of dogs and cats. Our research is focused on gatrointestinal function testing, gastrointestinal pathogens, and intestinal microbial ecology with an emphasis on probiotics and prebiotics and how intestinal pathogens lead to disturbances in the intestinal microbiota.*" *(See Book Chapter 6)*

Vilayanur S. Ramachandran and Lindsay M. Oberman in "Broken Mirrors: A Theory of Autism," Scientific American, November 2006 *(Book: Chapter 10)*

Wauquier, A. and Dugovic, C. Serotonin and Sleep-Wakefulness Annals of the New York Academy of Science Volume 600, The Neuropharmacology of Serotonin pages 447–458,October 1990 17 DEC 2006 DOI: 10.1111/j.1749-6632.1990.tb16901.x (Book: Chapter 12)

Yerkes RM, Dodson JD (1908). "The relation of strength of stimulus to rapidity of habit-formation". Journal of Comparative Neurology and Psychology 18: (459–482) *(Book: Chapter 1)*

DVDs

Canine Emotional Detox, by Diane Garrod www.tawzerdogs.com

Websites

Canine Transformations Learning www.caninetlc.com

Canine Transformations Learning Facebook business page www.facebook.com/cTLC3

Cascade, Kathy, Tellington Touch instructor and former physical therapist http://www.spiritdog.com/resources.htm

K9 Conditioning – http://www.fitpaws.com

Mayo Clinic, "Stress: Constant Stress Puts Your Health at Risk" (Book: Chapter 1) http://www.mayoclinic.com/health/stress/SR00001

Nutrition Data http://nutritiondata.self.com/foods-00007900000000000000.html (information on which meats contain tryptophan)

Ottosson, Nina, intelligence puzzles and games http://www.nina-ottosson.com/

Oxford Dictionaries – definition, reactive – http://oxforddictionaries.com/us/definition/american_english/reactive

Tellington Touch http://www.tellingtontouch.com (information on wraps, obstacle coursework, two-points of contact leading

Through a Dog's Ear http://www.throughadogsear.com

Thundershirt http://www.thundershirt.com

Vet Info, Dog Sleep Patterns https://www.vetinfo.com/dog-sleep-patterns.html

White, Jennifer, i2iK9 and Laughing Dog http://www.i2ik9.com/Staff.htm

YouTube References

Chai, mixed breed, fearful, no decision is also information. Part One: https://www.youtube.com/watch?v=rUSM6Yxi8gs&feature=youtu.be and Part Two: https://www.youtube.com/watch?v=XgsFpVwf_qE&feature=youtu.be Videos showing a dog who couldn't solve a problem

Dubois, Lyn, and her dog Tammy (Belgian Tervuren) advanced concept of size recognition. Concept of Tallest and Concept of smallest (https://www.youtube.com/watch?v=eIfHiiPAmW0)

Garrod, Diane YouTube Channel https://www.youtube.com/channel/UCUvQ2HCfmCF7vBfcdMW__0w

Harley the unreliable Pitbull https://www.youtube.com/watch?v=ces_dHqFLHk A video showing clear stress signals and worrisome behavior.

How to take resting respiratory rate (breaths per minute), VCA Animal Hospitals https://www.youtube.com/watch?v=uEptzj6G-Jk

How to take a dog's temperature https://www.youtube.com/watch?v=cXjg77ShJbM

Jack, Severe Separation Anxiety *(Book: Chapter 8)* A brief video of Jack pre-CED. This is what he would do all day, and this video is one of milder ones. https://www.youtube.com/watch?v=g4R1dEyG8eI

Max, English Bulldog and Basket Challenge – (https://www.youtube.com/watch?v=EKAbQpABtaw) a favorite problem-solving activity of clients and trainers

Music for dogs (there are many choices, so simply do a YouTube search)

Urinary pH informational, Karen Becker, DVM https://www.youtube.com/watch?time_continue=3&v=ZAy_KKRzJjo

What is a normal canine temperature reading https://www.youtube.com/watch?v=3z8ptw3Qj5g

About the Author

Diane Garrod is a PCT-A (professional canine trainer – accredited), with a degree in Communication and Journalism from University of Wisconsin. Garrod is a Founding Member of the Pet Professionals Guild: the association of force free pet professionals (PPG). She is Owner of Canine Transformations Learning, Langley, Washington (celebrating 11 years, January 2018), awarded 2016 and 2017 Best Business category Dog Trainer by Langley, WA Awards Committee.

Garrod has skills certifications in resource guarding, animal behavior, theriogenology, writing for the sciences, fear in dogs and cognition and emotion. Most recent certifications are in predation and aggression, 2017; and Aggression in Dogs: Safety, Defensive Handling, and Training 2017, as well as Fear Free Certification, through VetFolio by Marty Becker, DVM (fear free veterinarian practices) 2017. She is also a Guild Certified Tellington Touch Practitioner since 2011.

Garrod's main areas of research include stress in dogs and is the creator Stress Matters; the Canine Emotional Detox: Systematic stress release protocol for challenging canines. She is an international speaker on this topic and on solving the aggression puzzle, force free.

Garrod trains and competes in Rally-O, Rally-O Freestyle, Treibball (Certified Instructor and Judge, American Treibball Association (ATA), Barn hunting. She offers classes and workshops in Treibball, puppy growth privates, confident transformations for fearful dogs, four levels of reactive dog classes, privates in aggression and reactivity issues (dog dog, dog human, combination of both, environmental sensitivities and more) with recent addition of teaching service dogs to get their public access certification studying through Service Dog Training Institute (SDTI) Canada.

Garrod is a blog contributor for PPG World Services http://ppgworldservices.com/2015/05/08/can-you-fix-my-dog/ <http://ppgworldservices.com/2015/05/08/can-you-fix-my-dog/> and Blogspot with A Day in Life of Behavior Trainer blog: http://dayinthelifeofabehaviortrainer.blogspot.com/ <http://dayinthelifeofabehaviortrainer.blogspot.com/> web:

Garrod is a regular contributor to PPG's Barks from the Guild Magazine having cover articles in:

Dodging Euthanasia with Force Free techniques, a story about her own rehomed adoptee, Skye (mini-Australian Shepherd) who had a five-bite history sending owner to ER and ending up in quarantine with euthanasia on the table scheduled for next day. http://www.petprofessionalguild.com/event-2326495 <http://www.petprofessionalguild.com/event-2326495> Sept 2016, and 2017 Cover Article Multi-Dog Households Fighting protocol, a how-to in working through issues in a multi-dog household fighting situation.

Garrod has a DVD feature, 2015 www.tawzerdog.com <http://www.tawzerdog.com> on The Canine Emotional Detox: Systematic Stress Release Protocol for Challenging Canines.

Working teacher dogs Belgian Tervuren, Kody Bear, CGC, RN, BS, MA, former Therapy Dog with Love on a Leash program; Treibball Novice. Belgian Tervuren Valor, RallyO Freestyle, RallyO and Treibball Novice in-training. Both dogs are my partners in helping dogs and their owners transforming problems into positive solutions; RIP Belgian Tervuren, Chancellor April 3, 2004 to January 2015, the inspiration for the CED. New dog: Skye, mini-australian shepherd doing barn hunting, aggressive dog in-training (COVER story: Barks from the Guild - Dodging Euthanasia - all force free) FB page Skye blue skies from now on.

email to: garrod@whidbey.com or info@caninetlc.com

Website: www.caninetlc.com <http://www.caninetlc.com>

Email: info@caninetlc.com and garrod@whidbey.com

Phone: 360-320-9251

FB biz site: www.facebook.com/cTLC3 <http://www.facebook.com/cTLC>